9/94

D1154693

WITHDRAWN

Willa Cather

Willa Cather
Landscape and Exile

Laura Winters

SUP

Selinsgrove: Susquehanna University Press
London and Toronto: Associated University Presses

Associated University Presses
440 Forsgate Drive
Cranbury, NJ 08512

Associated University Presses
25 Sicilian Avenue
London WC1A 2QH, England

Associated University Presses
P.O. Box 38, Port Credit
Mississauga, Ontario
Canada L5G 4L8

The paper used in this publication meets the requirements of the American National Standard for Permanence of Paper for Printed Library Materials Z39.48–1984.

Library of Congress Cataloging-in-Publication Data

Winters, Laura, 1957–
    Willa Cather : landscape and exile / Laura Winters
       p.   cm.
    Includes bibliographical references and index.
    ISBN 0–945636–56–3 (alk. paper)
    1. Cather, Willa, 1873–1947—Criticism and interpretation.
2. Landscape in literature.   3. Exiles in literature.   I. Title.
PS3505.A87Z9384   1994
813'.52—dc20   92–51002
                                            CIP

For Joan and Donald Winters
and in memory of
Isabel Booth Greenhalgh

Tell me the landscape in which you
live and I will tell you who you are.
—José Ortega y Gasset

Contents

Acknowledgments

VI

A tune beyond us as we are,
Yet nothing changed by the blue guitar;

Ourselves in the tune as if in space,
Yet nothing changed, except the place

Of things as they are and only the place
as you play them, on the blue guitar,

Placed, so, beyond the compass of change,
Perceived in a final atmosphere;

For a moment final, in the way
The thinking of art seems final when

The thinking of god is smoky dew.
The tune is space. The blue guitar

Becomes the place of things as they are,
A composing of senses of the guitar.
—From "The Man with the Blue Guitar"
by Wallace Stevens

During the research, writing, and completion of this project, the following people have enriched my life by transforming ordinary space into the most sacred of places:

my parents, Donald and Joan Winters, who made my way easier with the precious gift of their love and support;

Brian, Angela, Rebecca, Courtney, and Sarah Winters, who often opened their home to me and provided me with a place full of love;

Jane and Ken Cole, who keep getting wiser but never any older;

Ann Sobine, Cindy Shogan, Joan Lucia, Elaine Hickey, Delia Gerace, and Claudia Myers, who teach me what friendship is;

Sister Eileen Kelly, who provides a loving, Spirit-filled model of fidelity;

my colleagues at the College of Saint Elizabeth, particularly Sister Jacqueline Burns, Sister Anne Haarer, Sister Ellen Joyce, George Sirgiovanni, Sister Jean Hemmer, Kathleen Hunter, John DeBenedetto, and Margaret Roman, who supported me in word and deed;

Chris Bruno and Sheila Thimba, who helped get the work done at vital moments;

Susan Rosowski, whose generous and insightful comments on this manuscript made the work stronger in every instance;

John Murphy, whose years of dedication to Cather studies guides us all;

Merrill Skaggs, whose scholarship, friendship, and wisdom directed this work from its beginning;

Sister Alice Lubin, whose gentle example of intelligence, compassion, and charity continues to enrich my life;

and in memory of Louis John Lubin, who shared with me his decency, integrity, and care. For the help of all of these people, I am deeply grateful.

Willa Cather

Introduction

I

This is a work about the ways in which Willa Cather transforms secular space into sacred places in her fiction. She uses landscape not merely as a backdrop against which her characters struggle but also as a dynamic presence and a character in her fiction. Place is, like consciousness, that which surrounds us always. Her characters run from it and escape into it. It involves both presence and absence; it is both empty and full. It may inspire pity, loathing, awe. Cather describes the way in which places allow people to understand their authentic selves. Cather's characters do not simply live in places; they *live* places emotionally, spiritually, and intellectually. Edith Lewis, Cather's companion of forty years, explains, "She saw the country, not as pure landscape, but filled with a human significance, lightened or darkened by the play of human feeling."[1]

In Cather's fiction landscape is destiny, as seen in her characters' obsessive need to root themselves in a particular landscape, in their inability to escape from the demands of a beloved place, and in their absolute need to move between the demands of at least two places.

No theorist of space can write without acknowledging a debt to Gaston Bachelard, particularly his ground-breaking

3

text, *The Poetics of Space*, in which his investigations "seek to determine the human value of the sorts of space that may be grasped, that may be defended against adverse force, the space we love."[2]   Bachelard is particularly interested in "the house as a *tool for analysis* of the human soul" and in smaller units, what he calls "houses of things: drawers, chests, and wardrobes."[3]   He asks fundamental questions helpful in any exploration of Cather's treatment of space and place: "How can an image, at times very unusual, appear to be a concentration of the entire psyche? How—with no preparation—can this singular, short-lived event constituted by the appearance of an unusual poetic image, react on other minds and in other hearts, despite all the barriers of common sense, all the disciplined schools of thought, content in their immobility?"[4] Bachelard's rhetorical questions remind Cather's readers of the power of her images of natural landscapes and of architectural structures. Cather's poetic images react on our minds and tease us until we must make sense of them.

The critical work nearest in spirit to this study is Judith Fryer's fascinating text, *Felicitous Space: The Imaginative Structures of Edith Wharton and Willa Cather*, which—in turn—relies on Bachelard's theories. While we deal with several of the same texts, our methods of considering issues of space (and, for me, the sacred place) are very different. Fryer's feminist analysis of the physical structures in Cather's fiction attempts to define the woman writer's method of responding "to the double bind of muteness, on the one hand, and the restricted language of the dominant culture, on the other."[5]   She is concerned with the interconnection between the woman writer's body, her voice, and the topographical structures she describes. In a key chapter, "Body, Memory, Architecture," concerning the power of landscape for Thea Kronborg and Jim Burden, Fryer's prose seems closely related to dream, to poetry. While her work is an interesting critical meditation on the nature of space in Cather's fiction, Fryer's feminist reading of Cather is not primarily interested in issues of space and place that derive fundamentally from the human condition rather than the gender of the character or writer. I am more interested in the impact of *exile* from a beloved landscape on Cather's characters.

Because I also believe one needs to recognize the demands of multiple landscapes as they appear in Cather's fiction, my analysis relates space and place to Cather's lifelong acknowledgment of the opposing forces that drive and determine character and action.

Hermione Lee's brilliant study, *Willa Cather: Double Lives*, is particularly helpful in acknowledging and charting the power of doubling and opposition in Cather's work. Lee contributes an eloquent analysis of specific Catherian pairs: "Cather's work gets its energy from contraries. She is pulled between the natural and the artificial, the native and the European. She is a democrat and an élitist. She relishes troll-like energy and primitivism as much as delicacy and culture. She is religious and fatalistic. She is equally interested in renunciation and possessiveness, in impersonality and obsession. Her fictions are of split selves and doublings. Above all, there is a paradox for Cather in the act of writing itself."[6]

Pablo Neruda has said of Walt Whitman, he "was the protagonist of a truly geographical personality: the first man in history to speak with a truly continental voice."[7] Willa Cather is the first American woman to speak with that same kind of voice. Like Whitman, she deliberately blurs the distinctions between self and place. Unlike Whitman, however, Cather has a geographical *imagination*. Her characters are intricately connected to the places they inhabit. Bartley Alexander cannot be fully understood apart from the kind of bridges he constructs, nor Marian Forrester apart from the rooms she inhabits, nor Godfrey St. Peter apart from the houses he chooses and rejects, nor Myra Henshawe apart from the interiors she creates and the cliff she travels to in order to die, nor Father Latour apart from the cathedral he builds and the cave he visits, nor Cécile and Euclide Auclair apart from the home they fashion, nestled into the rock of Quebec: the place of exile that they make their own. Cather's artistic voice speaks for and through the landscapes she loved, and her imagination works by opposition, furiously spinning doubles of character, experience, temperament, and place. Locating the scenes she imagines in particular places, she forces her readers to merge character and place in a way no American writer has done before or since.

II

In the Great Plains the vistas look
like music, like Kyries of grass . . . [8]
—Gretel Ehrlich

In *My Ántonia*, Jim Burden reads and translates a passage from the *Georgics* of Virgil:

> *"Primus ego in patriam mecum . . . deducam Musas"*; "for I shall be the first, if I live, to bring the Muse into my own country." Cleric had explained to us that "patria" here meant, not a nation or even a province, but the little rural neighborhood on the Mincio where the poet was born. This was not a boast, but a hope, at once bold and devoutly humble, that he might bring the Muse (but lately come to Italy from her cloudy Greek mountains), not to the capital, the *palatia Romana*, but to his own little "county"; to his father's fields, "sloping down to the river and to the old beech trees with broken tops."[9]

Jim learns that the poet's task is to breathe life into his native land. Cather uses an epigraph from Virgil for *My Ántonia*— *"Optima dies . . . prima fugit"*—and she repeats that passage ("the best days are the first to flee"), which Jim calls a "melancholy reflection" (*MA* 263). It is clear that giving a voice to one's beloved land and finding a voice with which to describe the precious days of youth are predominant concerns in Cather's *oeuvre*. In a series of letters, written over a thirty-year period to Carrie Miner Sherwood (*My Ántonia* is dedicated to Carrie and her sister Irene), Cather vividly recalls the intensity of her early experiences in the Miner's store and discusses her need to write fiction that will sound accurate to her Red Cloud neighbors. The sincerity of these letters betrays no ironic intention. Cather was interested in revealing the dark side of small town life, but these letters attest to the fact that she cared very deeply about the responses of her family and friends from Red Cloud. On one important level, she suggests, she is always writing for them.[10]

Frederick Turner, using the techniques of the cultural historian and the biographer, has written *Spirit of Place: The Making of an American Literary Landscape*, a work that describes writers "who learned in loneliness and silence and deprivation how truly to see where on the American earth they were: to see their specific places in such full and luminous detail that a radically native art, a literature arose."[11] Turner discusses the work of Thoreau, Twain, Cather, Sandoz, Faulkner, Steinbeck, Williams, and Silko. He says of Cather's need to describe the prairie, "this land, whatever else it was, was simply too big and powerful to be met without the mediating presence of a language, and she set out early to devise her own."[12]

My work is also an attempt to come to terms with important aspects of the language and technique Cather employs to describe landscape. Turner suggests that the artist who wishes to come to terms with personal identity in relation to landscape must learn how to see the beloved place "imaginatively enough and comprehensively enough so that its prosaic defects could become" its "best creative assets."[13] Turner uses a phrase that is especially applicable to Cather's fiction. He speaks of the artist's need to create a "mythic geography,"[14] by which a reader may recognize fundamental patterns of human experience in places particularly beloved of the artist. Cather successfully uses the Nebraska prairie, the topography of the American Southwest, and the rock of Quebec as her mythic geography. In these places, Cather's characters find a reflection of their interior states, a way out of their dilemmas, and powerful memory of their beloved alternate landscapes. Cather's mythic geography both encodes and resolves issues of exile. While all of Cather's novels include issues of exile, I am most interested in the brilliant novels written between 1923 and 1931, the most profoundly productive period in Cather's career. A close reading of *A Lost Lady, The Professor's House, My Mortal Enemy, Death Comes for the Archbishop,* and *Shadows on the Rock* establishes ways to understand Cather's treatment of exile that may also be used to read *Lucy Gayheart* and *Sapphira and the Slave Girl.*

Enlightening biographies by E. K. Brown (completed by Leon Edel), James Woodress, and Sharon O'Brien suggest that Cather's exile from the beloved Virginia of her childhood was the primary emotional event in her life. Through this experience, Cather learned to live in exile, and she kept repeating this familiar pattern throughout her life. At key turning points, an anxious Cather was forced to leave beloved places (Virginia, Lincoln, Pittsburgh, Bank Street) for unknown spaces. Cather's experience of place reflects what writer Italo Calvino has said of his own life of exile: "The ideal place for me is the one in which it is most natural to live as a foreigner."[15] Cather's fiction describes those foreign places in which human beings must begin to construct a life.

In *Placeways: A Theory of the Human Environment*, E. V. Walter introduces the term "topistics" as "a nonfragmentary theoretical framework to grasp the whole experience of place and space. Topistic inquiry seeks theories that represent and explain forces that make or break the integrity of located experience."[16] Walter suggests that we all

> build a structure of consciousness by supporting the features of experience that we acknowledge. We make the obvious world by building it, and in constructing the world, we build ourselves, including our structure of consciousness. We build to support certain features of experience and to suppress others, and these decisions to acknowledge or deny them give form to the dominant structure of consciousness.[17]

While he describes the way in which individuals and cultures literally build structures, Walter's theory helps explain the relationship between Cather's fictional structures (the locations her characters inhabit) and her artistic concerns. Walter suggests that although topistics is a neologism, it belongs "to ancient wisdom."[18] For him, a place is "a location of experience."[19] Because Cather believed firmly in that ancient wisdom, it is impossible even to imagine her characters apart from the places they inhabit. Thus in this study I will attempt to apply topistics to a reading of Cather's spaces that become transformed into sacred places when characters so identify with their resonance that the line between self and environment begins to dissolve.

In Cather's fiction, the sacred place is not always a place of peace and contentment. In fact, it may be the place in which one must come to terms with the most difficult unresolved impulses. The sacred place can be a place of danger because it is a place of transformation; it is liminal space. A sacred place reconciles opposites. A cliff, cave, mesa, garden, or cathedral is a reminder of the presence of the Spirit, of something larger than the self. Cather came to this experience of immanence very early in her life. In letters written when she was in her fifties, Cather describes the first days after her move to the Nebraska prairie. She suggests that she had to have it out with the landscape. Her antagonist became her lifelong friend.[20]

Cather depicts this struggle and reconciliation in the first section of *My Ántonia*. After his train journey, when Jim arrives in the boundary-less prairie, he feels as if he "were outside man's jurisdiction" (*MA* 7). In this limitless space, Jim feels "erased, blotted out" (*MA* 8). As the terrain surrounding his new home becomes more familiar, Jim, like Cather, comes to love the idea of place, the earth itself. As he explores his grandmother's garden, Jim experiences a moment of connection with the land itself:

> I kept as still as I could. Nothing happened. I did not expect anything to happen. I was something that lay under the sun and felt it, like the pumpkins, and I did not want to be anything more. I was entirely happy. Perhaps we feel like that when we die and become a part of something entire, whether it is sun and air, or goodness and knowledge. At any rate, that is happiness; to be dissolved into something complete and great. (*MA* 18)

The fact that the last part of this quotation is the epitaph on Cather's tombstone suggests the importance of the experience for her.

Soon after the publication of *Shadows on the Rock*, a profile of Cather, written by Louise Bogan, appeared in the *New Yorker*. Bogan says of Cather, "She is a writer who can conjure up the look of a place."[21] Cather does much more than that. She uses the description of the search for the sacred place to express the deepest longings of the human heart. For instance, during Tom Outland's halcyon summer of protection and connection with Roddy Blake, Rapp, the foreman of the Sitwell Company, warns the men not to try to enter the alluring mesa. This warning only fires Tom's imagination. He remarks, "I had my eye on the mesa all summer and meant to climb it."[22] In Cather's fiction, to locate oneself in relation to a place is to be fully alive, and forbidden places are often the most appealing.

This study of Cather is designed to accomplish what Yi-Fu Tuan suggests is the goal of all humanistic inquiry: "to increase the burden of awareness."[23] When considering Cather's fiction, the careful reader must be aware of Cather's intense examination of space and place. She must ask herself the questions Edgar Anderson asks in his essay, "The Considered Landscape":

> When we consider a landscape what *are* we considering? Is it just what we see or is it something more—if so, what is that something more? What we see is a view, most certainly. When we talk about landscape, when we try to have a meeting of minds as to its various problems, there is more than the view itself. We are contemplating what is before us. The eye is seeing and the mind is perceiving. What we think, what we ask, what we investigate will depend upon how rich is the experience brought to bear on that contemplation. It is not only what we see, it is also what we see *in* it.[24]

III

"All human history is the record of an emigration": about one hundred years ago, in June of 1890, Willa Cather delivered these words in her powerful address to her high school graduating class in Red Cloud, Nebraska.[25] This phrase, written when she was only sixteen, would reverberate in her mature fiction. Although her high school address is filled with inflated rhetoric, she movingly describes the inevitable "pilgrimage of humanity,"[26] the journey that defines us as human.

Willa Cather's life involved a series of key exiles and emigrations, both voluntary and involuntary. Her biographers all record the painful and exhilarating tension she felt between the demands of home and the excitement of journey. Any analysis of Cather's use of space and place must address this fundamental dichotomy and opposing pair of needs. James Woodress chooses to begin his definitive biography by showing Cather on a train platform, anxiously awaiting her next journey.[27]

In his anecdotal chapter on Cather's beloved Santa Fe, Frederick Turner touches on this opposition when he speaks of Cather's childhood exile from Virginia to Nebraska: "It was as if she were now overwhelmed by a feeling for two landscapes."[28] Cather's most penetrating literary creations and her most powerfully described characters enact this painful tension between the desire to hold on to a place that is beloved, in which one may abide, and the desire to travel, to break away. Each of Cather's characters must live with this painful dilemma. Cather's essay on Katherine Mansfield betrays her own intensity of feeling concerning the paradox of home and journey: "Always in his mind each member of these social units [families] is escaping, running away, trying to break the net which circumstances and his own affections have woven about him. One realizes that human relationships are the tragic necessity of human life; that they never can be wholly satisfactory, that every ego is half the time greedily seeking them, and half the time pulling away from them."[29]

Willa Cather's fiction is suffused with the notion of exile. Her characters, often banished from a native or authentic landscape (consider Jim Burden, Myra Henshawe, Tom Outland, Godfrey St. Peter, Bishop Latour, Euclide Auclair, Sapphira Colbert, among others), are restless pilgrims who long for home: a comforting space, a place to come to, a rest from the arduous journey.[30] In Cather's fiction, homemaking and "homesteading are activities which build a space where souls can thrive and dream—secure, protected, related, nourished, and whole."[31] Almost every major Cather character must, at some point, come to terms with the dilemma of exile from a beloved landscape.[32] To manage the condition of exile, Cather's characters must transform mundane (or what I call secular) spaces into sacred places. In these sacred places, existence suddenly makes sense; order is created from chaos; the history of the earth and the history of the individual merge and are reconciled. These sacred places bring peace: an aura of resolution and rightness pervades the very air.

Cather correctly indicates that these moments in a sacred landscape are very rare and that the demands of community will, at every turn, attempt to deprive us of them. The inviolate place is always violated. Our lingering in the place of the sacred is brief but vital to our very selves as human. Her characters' work is often the delicate and demanding construction of those sacred places. In *Death Comes for the Archbishop*, Latour attempts to reconcile the dichotomy between the quest for the creation of the sacred place and the demands of living in community. The cathedral he commissions draws the faithful into a sacred place dedicated to transcendence.

Cultural geographer Yi-Fu Tuan employs the term "topophilia" to discuss attachment human beings often feel for certain places.[33] We find self-definition by relating ourselves to place. Tuan makes a useful distinction between the arbitrary spaces we find ourselves in and those places we consciously create to feel at home: "Space is transformed into place as it acquires definition and meaning."[34] Cather creates characters who must imbue the spaces they inhabit with value as a way to learn to live in exile.

For instance, Jim Burden understands the prairie of his childhood (to which he comes after being orphaned) by making the explicit connection between that experience and one woman he has loved. Jim Burden must transform boundaryless space into a meaningful place. In the introduction to *My Ántonia*, Jim meets a childhood friend on a train journey across Iowa (a train is, in much of Cather's fiction, the perfect combination of motion and stasis, pilgrimage and comfort). There the two make meaning out of their life experiences by defining Ántonia as the embodiment of the child's perception of small-town life on the prairie: "More than any other person we remembered, this girl seemed to mean to us the country, the conditions, the whole adventure of our childhood" (*MA* ii). Jim uses Ántonia to make the vast, threatening expanse of the prairie into a manageable, valuable, memory-laden place.

One of Cather's most frequently quoted passages serves as a forceful example of this need to impose order on threatening, chaotic space. As Jim Burden (whose experience of exile from a beloved childhood landscape closely resembles Cather's own) rides in the back of a rough wagon into the darkness of the vast prairie, he thinks, "There was nothing but land: not a country at all, but the material out of which countries are made" (*MA* 7). This far from childish perception defines Jim's burden and Cather's task: to make a sacred place (imbued with meaning) out of this ostensibly formless landscape. It is not long before Jim finds out that what had appeared to be without shape or complexity is actually an undulating terrain, filled with prairie dog towns and rattlesnakes.

Cather's characters are trapped in what Vivian Gornick calls the search for "the deepest self."[35] Her characters can only identify those selves through the creation of sacred places. Thea Kronborg finds in the landscape of the Southwest an objective correlative of her own intense longings. In *Literary Women*, Ellen Moers, one of the first critics to consider Cather's use of space and its relation to gender, calls Cather's description of Panther Canyon in *The Song of the Lark* "the most thoroughly elaborated female landscape in literature."[36]

Both Cather's male and female characters share this need to define and create sacred places. Following the work of Bachelard, Tuan calls these locations "intimate places." They are "places of nurture where our fundamental needs are heeded and cared for without fuss."[37] When residing in the intimate place of care a person "is able to respond to the immediacy of the world and see it with the fresh intensity of childlike eyes. The lasting affection for home is at least partly a result of such intimate and nurturing experiences."[38] Certainly Cather's fiction is suffused with moments when a character is nutured and protected in a safe environment: Dr. Archie takes care of the sick Thea in *The Song of the Lark* and the young Cather waits, safely protected from the storm outside, to witness the reunion of Nancy and Aunt Till in *Sapphira and the Slave Girl*.

For the exile who must always come to terms with the demands of a new location, landscape itself, like miracle in

Cather's fiction, is the flowering of desire.[39] The sacred place is one that allows a character to recognize the value of the physical landscape—a rich available world—and also to acknowledge the truth that the available world is merely a shadowy reflection of a world of desire. In the search for the sacred place, as in religion, seeking is finding. Quest is fulfillment.

In summary, this work focuses on several pervasive methods of dealing with space and place in Cather's fiction. Chapter 1 presents and explains the metaphors of cantilever and suspension in Cather's first novel, *Alexander's Bridge*. Chapter 2 addresses the relationship between sacred space and artistic inspiration in *A Lost Lady*. Chapter 3 deals with the pervasiveness of possession in Cather's fiction, particularly in relation to landscape in *The Professor's House*. Chapter 4 explores Cather's ballad of death in exile as presented in *My Mortal Enemy*. Chapter 5 examines Cather's play with movement and stasis in *Death Comes for the Archbishop*. Finally, Chapter 6 describes the condition of exile in *Shadows on the Rock*.

1
Alexander's Bridge: Willa Cather's Philosophy of Composition

It so happens that the work which is likely
to be our most durable monument, and to convey
some knowledge of us to the most remote posterity,
is a work of bare utility; not a shrine, not a
fortress, not a palace, but a bridge.[1]
> —Montgomery Schyler

Architecture, wrote Mies van der Rohe in the
1920's, "is the will of the age conceived in spatial
terms."[2]

In Willa Cather's novels, architecture may be understood as
the intent of the writer expressed in a spatial idiom. In her
first published novel, *Alexander's Bridge*, Cather introduces
the pervasive concern with the demands of physical space
that will characterize all of her fiction. An exploration of the
structures of space in Cather's work is not merely a way to
understand her ideas. Space—and particularly the way in
which secular space is transformed into sacred places—*is*
Willa Cather's subject.

In Cather's fictional universe, deep patterns of human
experience cannot be understood apart from a profound
exploration of the ways in which human beings create and

inhabit space. Just as the scholar of modernist art examines Pablo Picasso's early academic drawings for clues to his later masterpieces, so must the Cather critic look to *Alexander's Bridge* to understand the writer's artistic process, her recurrent themes, and her map of reading.

In *The Kingdom of Art*, Bernice Slote analyzes Cather's early work and acknowledges that by the time Cather published her first novel she had been writing seriously and publishing reviews, essays, short fiction, and poetry for nearly twenty years. By 1911, Cather was no stranger to controversy, no naïve artist simply testing her powers. *Alexander's Bridge* needs to be recognized as the mature product of a woman nearly forty who was attempting to set down her opinions on force and on geography.

As many critics, from Slote onward, have suggested, *Alexander's Bridge* is not a superb novel; it is a derivative, too self-consciously structured work in which Cather sometimes shows her insecurity. In fact, in a 1931 essay, written almost twenty years after the publication of *Alexander's Bridge*, entitled "My First Novel [There Were Two]," Cather herself tried to disown this novel, suggesting that the composing of it was "like riding in a park, with someone not altogether congenial, to whom you had to be talking all the time."[3] Cather may have denied the importance of her first novel because it revealed too many of the methods she would later refine.

David Stouck explains that there "is a distinctly literary or 'invented' quality to *Alexander's Bridge*, apparent when the book is compared to a novel like *O Pioneers!*; however, a literary quality to a novel is not in itself negative but rather indicates a different kind of writing."[4] Stouck is perfectly correct. When he uses the term "literary" to describe the novel, he means a work consciously shaped to an artistic end. At its best, *Alexander's Bridge* eschews a certain blatant form of realism, popular when the novel was published. But if we expand Stouck's term "literary," to define a work that describes the process of creating art and that sets the foundation for metaphorical structures of novels to come, then we may see more clearly how much Cather accomplishes in her first published novel.

If we attempt to read *Alexander's Bridge* as Doris Grumbach does in her introduction to a recent edition of *O Pioneers!*, we get what she calls "an interesting, if nonpersuasive, international novel in the manner of Henry James."[5] If we look only to the narrative about a successful bridge builder who is torn between his love for his patrician wife Winifred and his passion for Hilda, his Irish-born lover, we are bound to see the novel as at least a partial failure. But if, in retrospect, after reading all of Cather's fiction, we view the work not so much as a novel but as a primer for our reading of Cather's technique (as her philosophy of composition), we are allowed a fascinating glimpse into Cather's own thought processes, particularly concerning the spatial metaphors that will control her later fiction.

In her cogent introduction to the novel, Slote makes clear the pervasive existence of doubles, especially those alternate selves that lie within the mask we present to the public. She calls *Alexander's Bridge* a novel of "the divided self."[6] It is important to note that in Cather's fiction, architecture, geography, spatial metaphors, and landscape always reinforce her lifelong concern with doubleness and division.

Sharon O'Brien suggests, in her introduction to a recent edition of *Alexander's Bridge*, that the work reflects Cather's deep fear of expanding her range from the short story to the novel form. O'Brien believes that Cather describes the anxiety of the creator who "applies the methods he derived from designing bridges of average length to this oversized construction."[7] Although this reading correctly begins to identify the bridge with the creative product, O'Brien also calls the work a "rejection of male-identified views of the artist and the creative process."[8] While Cather was torn between the literary prescriptions of Sarah Orne Jewett and those of Henry James, the tension between those two ways of seeing was based on the inherent merits or limitations of each position and not fundamentally on gender. Cather's body of work is a testament to her ability to reconcile the conflicting literary voices she heard. Any reading that suggests that Cather chose to privilege literary mothers over literary fathers fails to acknowledge the appeal of male identification for Cather.

O'Brien concludes that in *Alexander's Bridge*, "Cather condemns the urge to dominate and shows that the desire, if expressed by the artist, paradoxically results in imperfect structures."[9] This assessment of Cather's assertion in the novel fails to take into account Cather's fictional obsessions. Much of Cather's work (particularly her later novels of genius) is a testament to her belief that the artist *must* control her material. Although Cather may respect the foundation on which the work of art is based (and the reader of Cather's acknowledged and unacknowledged sources of her novels may well question even that supposition), for her the task of the artist is to *establish* and *retain* full control over her material. Still, O'Brien provides a valuable framework in which to understand the ways Cather employs images of engineering and structure to define the artist's work, and she also leads us on productive paths to show that Cather discusses literary construction when she depicts Bartley Alexander's bridge building.

Cather critics need to use O'Brien's insights with caution. She suggests that Cather's first novel is a self-conscious "deconstruction of masculine aesthetics,"[10] which could free the woman artist to gather her own internal strength and create her own designs. Although O'Brien wisely encourages us to read the novel as a work about the creative process, we must remember that Cather remained faithful to what she herself would term a male aesthetic throughout her life. And we must acknowledge Cather's identification, at least professionally, with what she would have defined as "conventional" male values such as objectivity, stamina, fidelity, and endurance.

This is not to say that men have been the best readers of Cather's work. In an early review in *Smart Set* from December of 1912, H. L. Mencken criticizes Cather for the artificiality of her narrative structure: "it seems a banal device to send him [Bartley] out on his greatest bridge a moment before it falls. . . . This is not a working out of the problem; it is a mere evasion of the problem."[11] What we have the pleasure of knowing, which Mencken did not, is that Cather wasn't after a certain kind of narrative structure. She plays with climax, destroys it entirely, to show what she will *not* do. At the end of the novel, Bartley is dead, but his suspension bridge stands as the architectural reminder of Cather's understanding of the need for a recognition of doubleness of place. Mencken asks, "In real life how would such a man solve it [the need to chose between wife and lover] for himself ?"[12] He provides his own answer: "No doubt the authentic man would let the situation drift."[13] Apart from the inherent misogyny (and finally misanthropy) of Mencken's statements, he misses the point of Cather's fiction. In his suggestion that Bartley Alexander is not an authentic man (and God save us from Mencken's brand of authentic men), who might bow to the exigencies of the situation by visiting Hilda four or five times a year, Mencken's criticism underscores the fact that "a certain kind of realism" alone is not what Cather is after. Her work has often been criticized for its apparent lack of structure. Cather replaces conventional wisdom concerning narrative structure with the literal structures she creates within her novels. In a sense, Cather kills off Mencken's kind of question from her very first novel.

Alexander's Bridge is not primarily a novel about infidelity; it is primarily about the need to construct bridges. Bartley Alexander, as character, cannot be understood apart from the structures he builds. As early as 1912, Cather merges fictional self with architecture. Alexander is a robust, self-confident engineer who is described as a physical force. He is compared several times with a catapult. As a young man he had been given the opportunity to finish the work on a suspension bridge at Allway—a way to suggest that human beings must keep all ways open. His success at this task provides him with recognition, money, and the offer of more work. At the opening of the novel, Bartley is a prominent figure, well respected by his peers, with a secure marriage. He is working on Moorlock, "the longest cantilever in existence,"[14] across the St. Lawrence River.

Because Cather employed so many specific details of the construction and collapse of the Quebec bridge over the St. Lawrence, it is reasonable to wonder why she chose to invent the death of Bartley Alexander. Theodore Cooper (the consulting engineer for the Quebec Bridge and Cather's real-life model for Bartley) was not present at the 29 August 1907 disaster,[15] whereas Bartley Alexander is on the bridge during its collapse. The way Cather reinvents the story leads one to ask: What needs to be destroyed in Cather's scheme?

To understand Cather's technique, it is necessary to think about the difference between a *cantilever* bridge, in which a section of the structure is thrust from a single support (connected only to one side) and the *suspension* bridge, in which the span is connected by two supports. It is no coincidence that Cather chooses these structures: "A cantilever bridge has at least one section not supported at one end."[16] The cantilever analogy reveals the flaw that will destroy Bartley. He thinks one's passion must reside in only one place. He can't imagine the need to divide his emotional and physical energy between two places. Bartley Alexander's suspension bridge at Allway stands as his crowning achievement, while his experiment with a cantilevered structure collapses.

Cather provides a very important clue to the spatial structures of her later novels, particularly *A Lost Lady, The Professor's House, My Mortal Enemy, Death Comes for the Archbishop,* and *Shadows on the Rock,* in which her characters (all of whom are exiles from a beloved place) must reject the notion that one exists solely in a single landscape. Just as the cantilever bridge collapses because it is connected on only one side (the strain is too much), so any Cather character who is unwilling to exist in one landscape while simultaneously remembering the demands of another is bound to come to a horrible end or, at best, remain miserably unhappy. Cather rejects the architectural metaphor of the cantilever bridge, while she wholly embraces the necessity for successful suspension between two beloved places.

Bartley Alexander remains in bitter conflict with himself because he refuses to believe that the intense, bittersweet memory of youth (reawakened in his passion for Hilda) must coexist with the physical and emotional demands of middle age. Intellectually and emotionally he is like his doomed cantilever bridge, wishing to be connected on only one side, and refusing to acknowledge the necessity of connection in both Boston (his home) and London (his lover's home). This is not to say that Cather's metaphorical structure suggests that

Alexander has to remain Hilda's lover, but it does imply that he must stop denying his wish for her. He needs to acknowledge the importance of the youthful Alexander, about whom he thinks often, instead of trying to kill him off.

Near the conclusion of the novel, Bartley travels by train back through Allway, across his first bridge. There he remembers his youthful self, so full of energy and possibility. As he looks around his compartment, he sees unkempt travelers "doubled in unlovely attitudes" (*AB* 119). They come "to stand to him for the ugliness he had brought into the world" (*AB* 119). These doubled men are ugly because they remind Bartley of his own limitation and his confinement in too small a place. He is able to remember his youth in his middle age, but he is unable to accept his need to maintain a connection to a beloved place of memory. He continues to fight the impulse to connect with two places simultaneously, and his refusal to accept the need for doubleness eventually destroys him. Bartley Alexander is at an impasse, caught in horrible, paralyzing indecision.

Interestingly, Alexander has his moment of greatest happiness—his most intense reconciliation of past and present—alone on a transatlantic voyage. On deck, suspended between the demands of two places, he experiences contentment: "He felt released from everything that troubled and perplexed him" (*AB* 73). With this scene of emotional tranquility, Cather does not imply that escape from choices is a solution. In fact, much of her fiction testifies to the need to recognize the power of human choice. She suggests instead that productive suspension between two beloved places is the only successful solution for exiles, and she makes clear that we are all exiles from some authentic landscape, whether literal or figurative. On deck, Bartley is as close as he will come to the productive suspension that will characterize Cather's later protagonists.

When Bartley is about to leave for England on one of his trips to see Hilda, he speaks to Winifred about his state of mind: "It's like the song; peace is where I am not" (*AB* 70–71). This refrain is the musical equivalent of the cantilever bridge: a self thrust into space, hoping for stability. When Bartley believes he can find no peace within himself, can take no peace with him to an alternate landscape, he fails in a way Godfrey St. Peter, Bishop Latour, Father Vaillant, and Cécile Auclair will not. Cather's characters must internalize the metaphor of suspension, of existing firmly *and* precariously in at least two different landscapes. Peace is where no one will ever be, but several of Cather's most appealing characters (Tom Outland, Myra Henshawe, Jean Marie Latour, Cécile Auclair) enact, as Cather needed to herself, the search for the sacred place, which includes a recognition of the need for multiple landscapes. Bartley Alexander is on that collapsing bridge at the end of the novel, in part, because Cather must reject the metaphor of the cantilever and embrace the metaphor of suspension. Soon after the actual Quebec Bridge disaster, one critic expressed, in *Scientific American*, what many engineers were then feeling and what Cather describes in her first novel: "the suspicion which is staring every engineer coldly in the face, that there is something wrong with our theories of bridge design."[17]

As an artist, Cather lived in delicate suspension, never totally anchoring a work in one conclusion. In fact, her fiction was often criticized in the popular press for its lack of definite resolution. A better way to understand Cather is to read her body of work as a series of bridges between and among her novels. She would explore important topics, such as possession and exile, through several novels, often reversing a conclusion reached in one work. Emotional, geographical, and professional suspension was a way of life for Willa Cather. An acknowledgment of the demands of delicate suspension cuts to the very heart of Cather's techniques.

Twenty years after *Alexander's Bridge* was published, Cather wrote "My First Novel [There Were Two]." Although most read the essay as Cather's wise recognition that her true territory was Nebraska—the land she came to love in exile, the land that captured her preadolescent imagination, held on, and would not let go—critics have not yet suggested why Cather may have written the essay *when* she did.

The year 1931 was critical in Cather's life for several reasons. She published *Shadows on the Rock*, which would signal the end of her most productive period as a writer. In the years from 1922 until 1931, she published six novels, five of which

—*A Lost Lady*, *The Professor's House*, *My Mortal Enemy*, *Death Comes for the Archbishop*, and *Shadows on the Rock*— represent her profound depth of vision concerning the human condition in both its tragic and redemptive forms.

At the end of this burst of productivity, Cather found it necessary to renounce her own first novel. Why would she revisit the issue at this point in her life? It is possible that after Cather worked out doubleness of space in *Death Comes for the Archbishop* and *Shadows on the Rock*, she became painfully aware of the limitations of the language of engineering and of metaphors of cantilever versus suspension as she had presented them in *Alexander's Bridge*. In the essay, Cather suggests that her view of the novel is not shared by all her readers: "I still find people who like that book because it follows the most conventional pattern."[18] In fact, the novel's narrative is fairly predictable until the climax, but the metaphorical pattern Cather sets up is far from predictable. Her play with doubleness of space is innovative and prophetic of movements in her best work.

In writing *Alexander's Bridge*, Cather was grasping for a way to address the fundamental issues of space and place, of relation, of existential dilemma, of choice, of consequence in human action, and of fidelity to multiple landscapes that would suffuse her mature fiction. She rejects her early effort after she recognizes the insufficiency of the mechanical model. Not until Cather exploits the language and symbol system of the Roman Catholic church (by "exploit" I mean to suggest that she uses it for its evocative power and employs it to contemplate the depths of the human heart) does she find a metaphorical structure that can encompass the complexity of her ideas about doubleness of space. In her first novel, Cather uses architecture where she needs incarnation. She uses structure when she needs transubstantiation. The language of engineering works here as a literal way to represent the doubleness of space she will later manage through allegory in *Death Comes for the Archbishop*. Mechanical metaphors will not work for Cather once she tries to describe worship and exile.

In the essay itself, Cather provides important clues as to why she would reject her first published novel: "Soon after the book was published I went for six months to Arizona and New Mexico. The longer I stayed in a country I really did care about, and among people who were a part of the country, the more unnecessary and superficial a book like *Alexander's Bridge* seemed to me."[19] It is clear from Cather's statements about the power of the landscape and atmosphere of the American Southwest that in it she had found *le paysage moralisé*, her terrain of the heart, an authentic landscape that could serve as a profound objective correlative of human longing, as a private encoding system of female desire, and as a landscape imbued with sacramental power.

In a 1927 letter, published in *Willa Cather on Writing*, Cather describes the power the geography of New Mexico and Arizona exerted over her:

> The longer I stayed in the Southwest, the more I felt that the story of the Catholic Church in that country was the most interesting of all its stories. The old mission churches, even those which were abandoned and in ruins, had a moving reality about them . . . In lonely, sombre villages in the mountains the church decorations were sombre, the martyrdoms bloodier, the grief of the Virgin more agonized, the figure of death more terrifying. In warm, gentle valleys everything about the churches was milder. I used to wish there were some written account of the old times when those churches were built; but I soon felt that no record of them could be as real as they are themselves.[20]

By 1931, the perfect fit between Cather's obsessive themes as an artist and what she found in the landscapes and stories of the Southwest rendered *Alexander's Bridge* obsolete to her. The novel was no longer as powerful an embodiment of her concerns as she once thought it was. Although Cather questions the value of her early work, it remains a gold mine for those interested in her treatment of architecture, space, and place because it contains the structural foundation on which her later masterpieces would rest.

2
Outside the Bedroom Window: The Laugh of the Muse in Willa Cather's *A Lost Lady*

In *The Writing Life*, Annie Dillard says, "Writing every book, the writer must solve two problems: Can it be done? and Can I do it?"[1] These kinds of questions were particularly pressing for Willa Cather as she wrote *A Lost Lady* because she was composing a book about inspiration found, lost, and found again.

The intellectual and emotional center of the novel involves the troubling questions Cather poses about Marian Forrester's behavior: "What did she do with all her exquisiteness when she was with a man like Ellinger? Where did she put it away? And having put it away, how could she recover herself, and give one—give even him—the sense of tempered steel, a blade that could fence with anyone and never break?"[2] These questions are not merely reflective of Niel's limited or immature speculations; they are fundamental to Cather's exploration of the tensions between living in the world of flesh and blood and inhabiting "the kingdom of art."

A Lost Lady is Willa Cather's meditation on the creative process, her attempt to come to terms with the muse. In *A Lost Lady*, Cather creates a narrative that draws on the images, metaphors, and conventions of medieval romance in order to talk about longing for artistic inspiration and fear of its absence.

A Lost Lady is a compendium of ways to approach the muse, a helpful and guarded handbook of responses to her. Every image and detail can be read as part of a parable about sources of inspiration.

Here Cather also continues to refine the spatial idiom she has been developing since *Alexander's Bridge*. Willa Cather has a geographical imagination—that is, she creates and understands ideas and characters primarily and fundamentally in relation to the places they inhabit. In *A Lost Lady*, concerns about the creative process and issues of inspiration found and lost are explored through the places Niel and Marian inhabit and share.

Marian Forrester, a rich embodiment of the muse, represents an inspiration it is impossible to ignore. Of Niel Cather writes, "He came to be very glad that he had known her, and that she had had a hand in breaking him in to life. He has known pretty women and clever ones since then,—but never one like her, as she was in her best days. Her eyes, when they laughed a moment into one's own, seemed to promise a wild delight that he has not found in life. 'I know where it is,' they seemed to say, 'I could show you!'" (*AL* 171). Marian (her laugh particularly) is a guide to what is best and most beautiful and valuable in the world. Niel needs to learn aesthetic lessons about the paradox of beauty and about the refiner's fire of human suffering. Marian teaches Niel, among many other lessons, how to survive after the worst has happened.

Marian Forrester as muse is mother, teaser, potential lover, betrayer, as well as one in need who must be protected. Not until Cather acknowledges that the protection goes both ways, that the muse may have a self-destructive mind of her own and that for women writers particularly, the muse not only nurtures, she must be protected, as when Niel cuts the phone cord to save Marian from the town's response to her most candid revelations.

Cather, as we know, felt she had found her subject when we wrote *O Pioneers!* By 1922, she was wondering where that muse has gone and whether it would ever come back. By the early twenties, Cather feared that the muse she had brought to her native land had fled the scene.

In *The Voyage Perilous*, Susan Rosowski writes of how Mrs. Forrester is understood, and of the mystery she remains: "On the one hand, there is Niel, trying to possess Mrs. Forrester imaginatively, to see his ideal in her and to discover her secret; on the other hand, there is Mrs. Forrester, elusively separate, teasingly contradictory."[3] Through Cather's layering of image and symbol, Marian comes to represent what is best and worst in the muse.

In the early 1920s, the nurturing, protective muse becomes for Cather an unfaithful lover. The beloved source of inspiration is a betrayer. Cather uses the powerfully evocative image of a parent/caretaker figure abandoning herself to another as a way to describe the desolation of inspiration lost.

Cather creates the central scene of the novel (that is, Niel standing outside Marian's window, and Niel ready to bestow roses when he hears her laugh with Frank) to describe the artist figure in the act of creation, in the process of composition. In *After the World Broke in Two: The Later Novels of Willa Cather*, Merrill Skaggs suggests that "Though she punishes him for it, Niel's child's vision is one that peeps and spies at adult secrets, then recoils, traumatized by primal scenes."[4] In this scene, Niel stands for the artist, who longs to tell the painful truth, but who always, on some level, remains an observer, outside looking in.

In an interesting work called "Doubling and Incest/ Repetition and Revenge: A Speculative Reading of Faulkner," John T. Irwin writes of the artist's task: "It is precisely because [he] stands outside the dark door, wanting to enter the dark room but unable to, that he is a novelist, that he must imagine what takes place beyond the door. Indeed, it is just that tension toward the dark room that he cannot enter that makes that room the source of all his imaginings—the womb of art."[5] The image of Niel standing outside Marian's bedroom is a way to describe the dangerous area Cather inhabited as an artist who needed to decide whether to tell the truth about aging, about the disappointments of mid-life, about radical abandonment, and about betrayal. Cather had been the responsible and petted child/artist for longer than most get to inhabit that role. In the 1920s, she had to begin to invent a middle-aged self.

At the literal center of the novel the bedroom scene encapsulates the themes Cather addresses in regard to the muse. After Niel's experience of greatest betrayal, he finds "himself at the foot of the hill on the wooden bridge, his face hot, his temples beating, his eyes blind with anger" (*AL* 86). When Niel must ask the hardest questions about beauty and about inspiration, he is on the bridge to the Forrester place: "It was not a moral scruple she had outraged, but an aesthetic ideal. Beautiful women, whose beauty meant more than it said . . . was their brilliancy always fed by something coarse and concealed? Was that their secret?" (*AL* 87).

To laugh and sleep with Frank Ellinger is to bend to the demands of living in the world, to accommodate one's self to things as they are. Marian can do that and land on her feet, like the cat she is compared to. But for Cather the experience of living in the world does move one away from the exquisiteness of the cocoon one creates when writing. Cather uses the devastation inherent in the moment when we intuit and then know that someone we love is comfortably intimate with another in order to describe the painful need of a writer to live in the world she can't fully control. To recognize that the muse sleeps with and laughs with the Frank Ellingers and Ivy Peters of this world shakes to the core the very hierarchies of beauty and exquisiteness that Marian as muse has come to represent. Frank and Ivy may stand for D. H. Lawrence and Ernest Hemingway respectively (writers Cather loved to hate), so that *A Lost Lady* can also be read as a novel about the state of American fiction in the early twenties.

At a time of profound crisis in her writing life and in her personal life, Cather was asking these questions of the muse—What spring will feed my inspiration, and What coarseness is in me? Could that coarseness be envy, pride?

For Niel (and we can make our speculations about Cather), the heterosexual bedroom from which he is cut off is the source of both productive anger and inspiration. We may begin to ponder how much of Cather's fiction was written out of anger; certainly the topic of anger in Cather's fiction demands further study. We can imagine that powerful feelings of some kind prompted those moments of intense composition that Edith Lewis describes. Could it be that anger produced some of those periods of inspiration where stories suddenly showed themselves whole?

In the early 1920s Cather is thinking back to her initial moments of inspiration, inextricably linked to Mrs. Silas Garber, a woman whose "laugh made me happy clear down to my toes."[6] Mrs. Garber, the prototype for Mrs. Forrester, is overtly linked to inspiration. Cather is afraid she has lost the energy of the preadolescent, the drive, the force that keeps one creating. Susan Rosowski reminds us that "in later years Cather said that to write well, she had to get up in the morning feeling thirteen and going for a picnic in that grove [Mrs. Garber's]."[7]

In *A Lost Lady*, when Captain Forrester is away on the business that will ruin him financially, Niel rises early after sleeping lightly: "He had awakened with that intense, blissful realization of summer which comes to children in their beds" (*AL* 84). He moves through a perfect morning, newly washed, fecund, and inviting. The morning represents a spot of time, a moment of being when the universe suddenly seems whole, and body and spirit are connected without self-consciousness to the external world. Of course this transcendent moment is not to last. Niel will have his deepest experience of betrayal (when he realizes that Marian is sleeping with Frank) on that beautiful morning in that beautiful place.

In the early 1920s, Cather realized that she had to reevaluate her relation to her own writing. Cather writes of the genesis of this novel: "*A Lost Lady* was a beautiful ghost in my mind for twenty years before it came together as a possible subject for presentation. All the lovely emotions that one has had some day appear with bodies."[8] Marian is the embodiment of Cather's emotions about inspiration. Certainly Mrs. Silas Garber, a powerful ghost of Cather's youth, stayed in the writer's creative mind as an image of beauty and inspiration.

When Cather was visiting with the Hambourgs in Toronto, while finishing *One of Ours*, "she received a copy of the Red Cloud paper reporting the death of Mrs. Lyra Anderson [that is, Mrs. Garber, who had married again], in Spokane, Washington, on March 21, 1921."[9]

Try to imagine the scene: Willa Cather thinking about inspiration. A newspaper account of the death of an influen-

tial figure of beauty from her youth, whose name is Lyra.
Certainly it is possible to speculate that the connection of
Lyra to lyre (the instrument associated with the muse figure)
may well have been in Cather's mind.

Lyra Garber's story became powerful and necessary for
Cather when that beloved presence was finally lost to this
world. Edith Lewis suggests that the whole novel took shape
in several hours after Cather read the obituary because she
had found exactly the story of loss and betrayal that she needed at that moment. Paradoxically, in response to fear of loss
of inspiration, Cather writes what is considered by many one
of her best novels.

At a time when then world had broken in two, when Cather
was tired, threatened, overwhelmed, in danger of succumbing
to fatigue, resentment, bitterness, and depression, she fashioned a parable about inspiration found and lost. By 1922,
Willa Cather had every reason to write about lost ladies.
Isabelle McClung had moved to Europe, Ántonia and Alexandra and Thea were far behind her, and Cather wondered who
the new ladies would be. *A Lost Lady* then is a novel about
separation from the most profound sources of art.

In a way no less pervasive than in her other great works,
this novel is about exile from a beloved place of inspiration.
Cather describes powerful spaces in the novel in order to
define the muse and describe the creative process. The For-
resters are associated with the marsh, the house, the woods,
the bedroom, and the garden. Cather's willing and unwilling
exiles are framed and defined by the spaces they inhabit.

Niel is incomplete, in part, because he is not sure of his
place. When his father leaves Sweet Water in economic
defeat, Niel feels he "might as well stay there [in Sweet
Water] as anywhere" (*AL* 33). A person who is not sure of his
place is certain to be punished in Cather's fiction.

In *A Lost Lady*, place and character are inextricably bound.
At the beginning of the novel Cather provides over three pages
of description of place—of Sweet Water and of the Forrester
property itself—before she introduces Marian. Both Captain
and Mrs. Forrester are vitally linked to the places they inhabit.
Marian is associated with the sexualized marsh, with its
"thatch of dark watercress" (*AL* 16), and with the "deep ravine

that winds into the hills" (*AL* 65), in which Marian and Frank Ellinger make love. Cather's language for that ravine evokes the powerful images of ravines and mountain clefts from the Old Testament *Song of Songs*. Marian is also associated with the Sierras, where she goes as a young woman to escape sexual scandal. In the mountains, during an adventure with Fred Harney, a guide she persuades "to take her down the face of Eagle Cliff" (*AL* 164 – 65), Marian falls and is rescued by Captain Forrester. Of these mountains, representative, in part, of her passionate nature, Marian says, "The Sierras,— there's no end to them, and they're magnificent" (*AL* 163).

The Forrester house itself becomes a representative of the female body: "Stripped of its vines and denuded of its shrubbery, the house would probably have been ugly enough" (*AL* 10–11). This description begins to suggest the importance of covering, of artifice and of how Niel is simultaneously attracted to and repulsed by adult female sexuality.

While Niel lives "on the edge of the prairie" (*AL* 29), the Forrester home is "placed on the hill, against its bristling grove, it was the first thing one saw on coming into Sweet Water by rail, and the last thing one saw on departing" (*AL* 11). The Forrester land is central to the experience of Sweet Water: "To approach Captain Forrester's property, you had first to get over a wide, sandy creek which flowed along the eastern edge of the town. Crossing this by the foot-bridge or the ford, you entered the Captain's private lane, bordered by Lombardy poplars, with wide meadows lying on either side. Just at the foot of the hill on which the house sat, one crossed a second creek by the stout wooden road-bridge" (*AL* 11). To get to the Forrester place, one has to cross over—out of mundane time and space, into a new location, suspended from the moral and cultural demands of small-town Sweet Water.

Cather provides an explicit clue to her linking of issues of place, sexual betrayal, and the process of reading and writing at the beginning of the chapter in which Niel will move most radically from innocence to experience. Cather describes the young man's reading: "He had no curiosity about what men had thought; but about what they had felt and lived, he had a great deal" (*AL* 81). Being outside Marian's bedroom window acts as a metaphor for both reading and writing. Cather indicates that one form of "eavesdropping" is much like the other. Of Niel's reading Cather asserts, "He did not think of these books as something invented to beguile the idle hour, but as living creatures, caught in the very behavior of living,—surprised behind their misleading severity of form and phrase. He was eavesdropping upon the past, being let into the great world that had plunged and glittered and sumptuously sinned long before little Western towns were dreamed of" (*AL* 81–82). The act of reading itself is, for Cather, like standing outside, listening in. Niel must learn that his lady participates in the grand adventure of living. Cather as artist must learn that in order to write we must become human. We must eavesdrop on the worst. We must come to terms with the laugh of the muse.

Marian laughs at other key moments in the novel. One of the most prominent and disturbing examples involves betrayal: "One morning, Niel was coming up through the grove, he heard laughter by the gate, and there he saw Ivy, with his gun, talking to Mrs. Forrester. She was bareheaded, her skirts blowing in the wind, her arm through the handle of a big tin bucket that rested on the fence beside her. Ivy stood with his hand on his head, but there was in his attitude that unmistakable something which shows that a man is trying to make himself agreeable to a woman. He was telling her a funny story, probably an improper one, for it brought out her naughtiest laugh, with something nervous and excited in it, as if he were going too far" (*AL* 119). Marian is both appealing and infuriating because she mocks "outrageously at the proprieties she observed, and inherited the magic of contradictions" (*AL* 79). Cather's argument with the muse is embodied in Niel's anger with Marian: "It was what he most held against Mrs. Forrester; that she was not willing to immolate herself, like the widow of all these great men, and die with the pioneer period to which she belonged; that she preferred life on any terms" (*AL* 169). In the dangerous early 1920s, inspiration refuses to die. It wants to live, even though the frontier and the narratives of the pioneer spirit may no longer be Cather's central subjects.

In *A Lost Lady*, Cather returns to image patterns she established in her earlier fiction. In *Alexander's Bridge*, she sets up the companion metaphors of cantilever and suspension bridges. Her characters who survive must live suspended between and among their beloved landscapes (of memory and desire). In *Willa Cather's Modernism*, Jo Ann Middleton reminds us that "with *A Lost Lady* Cather rewrites her first novel on her own terms."[10] Here Middleton specifically addresses technique, particularly concerns of point of view she learns from James and Flaubert. But I suggest that in *A Lost Lady*, Cather rewrites the bridges from her first novel. Niel's reading "made him wish to become an architect" (*AL* 82). He is, in that way, reminiscent of Bartley Alexander.

There are no fewer than twenty references to bridges in this novel, and they come a key moments. Niel finds himself on the bridge to the Forrester place at his moment of greatest devastation, and he lives. The novel suggests that he is able to move forward.

On the stormy night when Marian comes to Niel at his uncle's law offices in order to call the newly-married Frank Ellinger, Marian says she had come "over the bridge, what's left of it" (*AL* 129). She has to cross over into the public sphere. At the most crucial moments in this novel, characters cross bridges to new insights and self-definitions.

Cather provides a powerful image of the delicate suspension one must engage in as artist. When Niel returns to Sweet Water after two years in the East, he returns to the Forrester place and experiences a bittersweet reunion with Marian: "Niel went round the house to the gate that gave into the grove. From the top of the hill he could see the hammock slung between two cottonwoods, in the low glade at the farther end, where he had fallen the time he broke his arm. The slender white figure was still, and as he hurried across the grass he saw that a white garden hat lay over her face. He approached quietly and was just wondering if she were asleep, when he heard a soft, delighted laugh, and with a quick movement she threw off the lace hat through which she had been watching him. He stepped forward and caught her suspended figure, hammock and all, in his arms. How light and alive she was! like a bird caught in a net. If only he could rescue her and carry her off like this,—off the earth of sad, inevitable periods, way from age, weariness, adverse fortune!" (*AL*

109–10). Finally, the muse, suspended above the demands of the powerful earth, laughs *with* Niel. For a moment he regains the muse in the very setting that had been so alive and powerful for him as a child. He lives for a moment in that place of creation—suspended with the muse in his arms.

During his first time in Marian's bedroom, the "little boy was thinking that he would probably never be in so nice a place again" (*AL* 28). This is the muse as protective, nurturing, caretaking mother, who is safely sexualized and nonthreatening. But as an adult, Niel can, for a moment, hold the muse above the demands of the earth in a beautiful grove where the past and present are suspended in her sweet laugh.

In her description of Captain Forrester's toast, Cather provides an invocation to the muse, a model of what the writer under siege must accomplish: "It was the toast he always drank at dinner, the invocation he was sure to utter when he took a glass of whiskey with an old friend. Whoever had heard him say it once, liked to hear him say it again. Nobody else could utter those two words as he did, with such gravity and high courtesy. It seemed a solemn moment, seemed to knock at the door of Fate; behind which all days, happy and otherwise, were hidden. Niel drank his wine with a pleasant shiver, thinking that nothing else made life seem so precarious, the future so cryptic and unfathomable, as that brief toast uttered by the massive man, " 'Happy Days'!" (*AL* 50–51). Captain Forrester may stand for the artist who recognizes the demands of the muse. He accepts her for what she is, embraces the muse in her limitations and is therefore willing and able to ask for happiness.

A Lost Lady is antimimetic. In every detail the novel is a parable about inspiration and about the creative process. In his moving poem "To Urania," itself a powerful response to a muse figure, Joseph Brodsky meditates on the interstices among space, absence, and the human body. He writes,

> And what is space anyway if not the
> body's absence at every given
> point?[11]

The absence of the nurturing muse in the early 1920s could have destroyed Cather. Instead that absence became the source of her most creative work. She used the challenge to attack the hardest subjects she could imagine. At this time, Willa Cather had to decide what kind of a writer she wanted to be. The marsh of her creative inspiration was being drained. As much as *Shadows on the Rock* is a novel about endings of centuries, of days, of summer, *A Lost Lady* is about a town no longer on the line, passed by, no longer central. Surely Cather was asking how to remain central and whether being central was a worthy aspiration. In this powerful novel, Cather examines the connections between infidelity and lack of inspiration. Marian's secret is that she is willing to settle for what is available. The novel ends with another invocation, Niel happy that Mrs. Forrester "was well cared for, to the very end" (*AL* 174). He is able to say, "Thank God for that!" (*AL* 174).

3
Landscape and Possession in
The Professor's House

I

The world broke in two in 1922 or thereabouts.[1]
—Willa Cather

The next four chapters concern the ways in which Cather transforms space into place in four novels written between 1925 and 1931. When she was forty-nine, the world broke in two for Willa Cather. Even her description of dramatic change is expressed in a spatial metaphor. For a writer already predisposed to find doubleness everywhere, human suffering represented a rift, a break in the world.

Because the world was now divided, the only way to inhabit that space was to be willing to live in two landscapes simultaneously. In a world divided by human suffering, loss, and betrayal, survival rested in acknowledging the need for doubleness. Fortunately, Willa Cather's life experiences had prepared her to live that kind of life and to write fiction about that painful dilemma. During 1925 to 1931, the six most productive years of her career as a novelist, Cather chose four narratives that would allow her to work out the possibilities of inhabiting two places at once. Her genius allowed her to turn a life-shattering blow into a triumph. Cather chose stories of the quest for the sacred place that demanded a recognition of the need for multiple landscapes.

This need to exist in a broken world led to what I call Cather's "pilgrim imagination." This way of seeing is inherent in many of Cather's important critical precepts: "Whatever is felt upon the page without being specifically named there—that, one might say, is created. It is the inexplicable presence of the thing not named, of the overtone divined by the ear but not heard by it, the verbal mood, the emotional aura of the fact or the thing or the deed, that gives high quality to the novel or the drama, as well as to poetry itself."[2] The "thing not named" suggests a doubleness, an absence and a presence. There exists the text itself and an alternate text created by the reader. Sarah Orne Jewett advised Cather that "One must know the world *so well* before one can know the parish."[3] The resonance of those words spoke to Cather, an artist whose creative mind was drawn to the need for exile and return.

In "Old Mrs. Harris," Vickie Templeton receives the following advice from Mr. Rosen: "Listen: a great man once said: '*Le but n'est rien; le chemin, c'est tout.*' That means: the end is nothing, the road is all."[4] This advice suggests the need for inevitable movement. In Cather's fiction, the road is all. Her characters are restless pilgrims searching for the sacred place. Four of Cather's best novels, *The Professor's House*, *My Mortal Enemy*, *Death Comes for the Archbishop*, and *Shadows on the Rock*, embody in theme, characterization, image pattern, and spatial structure the paradox of movement versus stasis. In Cather's fictional universe, to live at all is to feel the pull of multiple landscapes. While *One of Ours* involves related issues of exile, I am more interested in Cather's novels that directly address transcendent or religious experience.

Woodress writes, "by 1922 when the world was breaking in two, Cather began to feel the need for religion."[5] She manifested this need by joining, at least in name, the Episcopal Church in Red Cloud and by the choice of the stories she would tell, the novels she would write over the next nine years. The very notion of belief implies doubleness. One has faith in something one does not see. The believer has faith in an alternate universe, whether that be embodied as a place, as a being, or as a part of the self one needs to reach.

Any great artist creates as a way to answer the questions pressing most forcefully on her. Cather wrote her novels of the 1920s to answer the question: How can one live in a divided world?[6]

Cather's imagination is most attracted to those characters and situations that suggest a stranger inhabiting a world he or she must grow to understand. As a way to embody the quest for the sacred, the search for meaning that surrounds the life of a thinking person, Cather turned to landscape, to an exploration of the meanings inherent in places.

Mary Gordon's description of painter Edouard Vuillard's technique could well stand as an accurate description of Cather's fictional style: "[H]is quality of quiet dreaminess, the contemplative range of his palette, his ability to create narrative tensions using only hints, his struggles with fullness and emptiness of space represent the quiet, ambiguous anguishes and joys that are another part of being modern."[7] In her play with the demands of multiple landscapes, Cather provides a similar definition of what it is to be modern. Like Vuillard, Cather presents apparently tranquil canvases, which, on closer inspection, reveal the complexity just below the surface of ordinary life.

II

Because the task of any criticism concerning a writer's work is to simplify, to clarify a scheme that has been ever present but not fully recognized, this chapter considers a pervasive set of concerns that direct the structure, the character development, and the prevailing metaphors present in Cather's fiction. All her novels fundamentally concern possession. Each work presents a different version of the key question: What is it legitimate to possess?

We need only look to Cather's evocative titles to detect the profound influence on her work of that kind of question. There are at least three types of clues to possession in her titles. For *My Ántonia, One of Ours,* and *My Mortal Enemy,* Cather chooses titles that emphasize possessive pronouns to highlight the primary questions to be addressed in the novels: Who owns a person's story? How much is the community responsible for the development of character? From whose perspective do we gain knowledge of Ántonia Shimerda, Claude Wheeler, and Myra Henshawe?

In two other titles, Cather underscores her metaphorical structure by using a possessive noun to raise the question of ownership. In his definitive biography of Cather, James Woodress reminds us that *Alexander's Bridge*, originally titled *Alexander's Bridges*, was scheduled to appear in *McClure's* under the title *Alexander's Masquerade*.[8] In Cather's first novel, the image of the bridge acts as an analogy to the way the artist/lover must exist hanging over a dangerous gorge, always suspended between at least two conflicting impulses. The *Professor's House* could have been aptly named *The Professor's Houses* because of the vital importance of architectural structures as objective correlatives to the internal longings of Louie Marsellus, Godfrey St. Peter, and Tom Outland.

In her title, *The Song of the Lark*, Cather refers to a painting by Jules Breton, which she saw at the Art Institute of Chicago. In *The Voyage Perilous: Willa Cather's Romanticism*, Susan Rosowski suggests that *The Song of the Lark* is for Cather what *The Prelude* is for Wordsworth: a record of the development of the artist's consciousness.[9] In the painting to which the title refers, a young, robust woman on her way to or from the physical exertion of difficult harvesting looks up to hear the bird's song. In the novel, Cather asks how fully the artist is herself responsible for her creative impulse and her own genius. Cather questions whether one can ever possess one's own talent: does an understanding of inspiration remain always separate, haunting one as the song of the lark haunts the farm girl in the painting?

By emphasizing the ideals of childhood that seem always to be receding into the distance, *A Lost Lady* describes the excruciating emotional journey of Niel Herbert, who must recognize that his immature, chivalric image of Marian Forrester cannot be held onto without a dangerous and self-destructive movement into an illusory world. He must both lose and retain his lady.

Sapphira and the Slave Girl poses this question: Can one own a human being? Cather also asks a more subtle and complex question regarding possession here: Whose plot of Southern prejudice is it anyway? I am indebted here to Merrill Skaggs's work on *Sapphira*, which, in part, raises the question of how Cather's last completed novel undercuts the reader's conventional expectations of the behavior of male slave owners and the self-possession possible for a young slave woman.

While the titles of *O Pioneers!* and *Death Comes for the Archbishop* do not as overtly refer to possession, at the heart of each novel exists a fundamental question of ownership: who can possess the landscape (as in *O Pioneers!*) and how does one answer the charge to possess a diocese while at the same time working toward possessing and determining the direction of one's spiritual development (as in *Death Comes for the Archbishop*). Certainly the title *Death Comes for the Archbishop* suggests the power of death to overtake and possess us.

Lucy Gayheart and *Shadows on the Rock* as clearly address issues of possession as Cather's other novels do, although their titles don't specifically direct the reader to those concerns. Both works present daughters who must gain and maintain possession of virtue in worlds of cruel selfishness. *Lucy Gayheart* could be said to show the hazards of failing to possess one's beloved, one's own life, or one's landscape. *Shadows on the Rock* emphasizes the dear things one must possess to make a life. Cécile Auclair must also decide what home to take possession of.

This pervasive scheme of possession in the novels of Willa Cather is most forcefully worked out in *The Professor's House*. In that novel Cather asks questions about and arrives at very profound answers concerning what can be possessed of houses, of one's family happiness, of the artifacts of a bygone civilization, of control over one's time of death, of the patent on an invention, of the vitality of a student who reminds one of lost youth, and of the landscape itself.

III

> If our imaginative writers are correct, the
> landscape may be a decisive clue to the special
> character of American thought and behavior.[10]
>
> —Leo Marx

As a way to explain possession, Cather searched for meanings inherent in new landscapes. She also returned, imaginatively, to the meanings accruing in the old places she had loved. *The Professor's House* is full of meaning-laden places. As much as any other Cather novel, this work is about how place becomes important through association and use. Through her description of St. Peter's life's work, Cather provides the reader with a picture of how landscape is transformed into text. She says of Godfrey's *Spanish Adventurers in North America*, "[T]he notes and the records and the ideas always came back to this room [the attic]. It was here they were digested and sorted, and woven into their proper place in his history."[11] Like the beleaguered Professor Crane, who perhaps deserves more than he gets in reward for his help to Tom Outland, Cather is, in *The Professor's House*, performing "delicate experiments that had to do with determining the extent of space" (*PH* 141).

Early in the novel, the Professor is defined as an exile from the beloved lake of his childhood. St. Peter must, like many of Cather's protagonists, come to terms with exile. He creates a French garden in Hamilton, paradoxically, to remember his "home" in France: "[I]t was there he and Tom Outland used to sit and talk half through the warm, soft nights" (*PH* 15). For St. Peter, the garden, like the lake, is a place in which to "evade the unpleasant effects of change" (*PH* 15).

Lake Michigan represents for him the very idea of childhood itself: "It was the first thing one saw in the morning, across the rugged cow pasture studded with shaggy pines, and it ran through the days like the weather, not a thing thought about, but a part of consciousness itself" (*PH* 30). The lake provides what Gaston Bachelard calls "a form that guides and encloses our earliest dreams."[12] St. Peter is abruptly taken from that indwelling landscape:

> When he was eight years old, his parents sold the lakeside farm
> and dragged him and his brothers and sisters out to the wheat
> lands of central Kansas. St. Peter nearly died of it. Never could
> he forget the few moments on the train when that sudden, inno-
> cent blue across the sand dunes was dying forever from sight. It
> was like sinking for the third time. (*PH* 30–31)

This experience is the primary emotional event of St. Peter's
childhood. It determines (as her early acquaintance with exile
would for Cather) his adult actions in very important ways.

As a historian, St. Peter understands his work in relation to
place. Cather provides a key image in which self, work, and
place are intrically linked. With the help of his foster brother,
Charles Thierault, St. Peter sails from Spain and experiences
a moment of being in which the plan for his life's work coa-
lesces:

> On the voyage everything seemed to feed the plan of the work
> that was forming in St. Peter's mind; the skipper, the Catalan
> second mate, the sea itself. One day stood out above the others.
> All day long they were skirting the south coast of Spain; from
> the rose of dawn to the gold of sunset the ranges of the Sierra
> Nevadas towered on their right, snow peak after snow peak, high
> beyond the flight of fancy, gleaming like crystal and topaz. St.
> Peter lay looking up at them from a little boat riding low in the
> purple water, and the design of his book unfolded in the air
> above him, just as definitely as the mountain ranges themselves.
> And the design was sound. He had accepted it as inevitable, had
> never meddled with it, and it had seen him through. (*PH* 106)

A reader of Cather's criticism knows how close this conception is to Cather's own understanding of the relationship
between topography and the creative product. In discussing
Sarah Orne Jewett's work, particularly *The Country of the
Pointed Firs*, Cather describes the organic connection
between story and place: "The design is, indeed, so happy, so
right, that it seems inevitable; the design is the story and the
story is the design. The "Pointed Fir" sketches are living
things caught in the open, with light and freedom and air-
spaces about them. They melt into the land and the life of the
land until they are not stories at all, but life itself."[13] Here

Cather could well be describing her own technique in *The Professor's House*, and in her writing generally, in which character and setting and theme are inextricably bound. Cather believed, for instance, that in *O Pioneers!* the country itself kept insisting on being her hero.[14]

Cather repeats the key image of being aboard ship when she describes one of St. Peter's moments of deepest connection with his wife, which occurs while they attend the opera to see *Mignon* in Chicago. St. Peter suggests to Lillian that instead of having had a family and having become middle-aged, they "should have been picturesquely shipwrecked together" (*PH* 94). But when he later revisits that thought, he still imagines himself alone with his plans for *work*. In his fantasy of connection, "[N]obody was in it but himself, and a weather-dried little sea captain from the Hautes-Pyrénées, half a dozen spry seamen, and a line of gleaming snow peaks, agonizingly high and sharp, along the southern coast of Spain" (*PH* 95). Even in his moments of greatest desire for connection, St. Peter imagines himself essentially alone on water, planning the course of his intellectual life, within view of a meaning-laden landscape.

Once again in the novel, when St. Peter considers his personal crisis and the jealousy and greed of his daughters, his wife, and his colleagues, he imagines a very different kind of sea voyage:

> The university, his new house, his old house, everything around him, seemed insupportable, as the boat on which he is imprisoned seems to the sea-sick man. Yes, it was possible that the little world, on its voyage among all the stars, might become like that; a boat on which one could travel no longer. (*PH* 150)

St. Peter needs time away from the wreck of his family life. While in much of her fiction, Cather succeeded "in giving significance to the American westering experience,"[15] it is remarkable how much her characters need moments of stillness in a particular place, how much they need to be *not* moving.[16]

When his family is traveling in France, St. Peter daydreams as he relaxes near his beloved lake. In those dreams,

"Tom Outland had not come back again through the garden door (as he had so often done in dreams!), but another boy had: the boy the Professor had long ago left behind in Kansas, in the Solomon Valley—the original, unmodified Godfrey St. Peter" (*PH* 263). Alone with his own reveries in a perfectly inviting landscape, St. Peter attempts to reconcile his youthful self with the adult Godfrey St. Peter. He needs, as Tom Outland does, to find a place in the world, one that, for him, will accommodate both the youthful Godfrey and the middle-aged professor of history.

The beginning of the novel makes clear that Godfrey and his house will be intimately linked. The man and the structure cannot be separated. The defects of the house reflect St. Peter's physical and emotional state: "certain creaking boards in the upstairs hall, had made him wince many times" (*PH* 11). Cather presents six major houses through which her drama is enacted: Godfrey's old and new houses, Kathleen and Scott's bungalow, Rosamond and Louie's mansion, which they name Outland, Tom and Roddy's cabin, and Tom's home in the cliff city itself.

Even though Cather had already used the landscape of the Southwest, particularly the ancient cliff dwellings in *The Song of the Lark*, the broken world forced her back to that landscape. In *The Professor's House*, she places a sensitive and vulnerable male character in the landscape she had feminized and eroticized in *Lark*. Unlike Alexandra Bergson and Ántonia Shimerda, who (like Cather) need to come to terms with threatening, open space, Tom Outland and Godfrey St. Peter must learn to inhabit enclosed interior spaces. St. Peter becomes the madman in the attic, who must reconcile his conflicting impulses of isolation and the need for community. His relationship with Tom Outland provides him a mirror image of himself as a young man. Through his connection with his brilliant student, St. Peter is able to decide what he needs to possess.

Unlike Bartley Alexander, who refuses to acknowledge his youthful self, Godfrey longs for a state of being before the advent of what he calls "cruel biological necessities" (*PH* 21); he means passion. The drama of *The Professor's House* resides in St. Peter's acknowledgment "that adolescence grafted a new creature into the original one, and that the complexion of a man's life was largely determined by how well or ill his original self and his nature as modified by sex rubbed on together" (*PH* 266 – 67).

The Professor's suspension between his two houses reflects both his dilemma and his power. In *The Stuff of Sleep and Dreams*, Leon Edel reads *The Professor's House* as an allegory concerning the infantile need to possess the mother fully and live within what Edel refers to as "a cave of one's own."[17] This place of protection, this cave, is embodied in St. Peter's attic room that is supported by family but sufficiently separate from the suffocating concerns of daily family life. Edel reads this image and St. Peter's relationship with Augusta negatively as the Professor's failure to achieve healthy maturity. Another way to read the image would emphasize the Professor's wise refusal to capitulate fully to the adult Godfrey. His relationship with Tom Outland's landscape helps Godfrey remember his youthful self, and it allows him to maintain connection to a life-giving image of youthful energy. St. Peter suggests that teaching remains an interest because he continues to be in thrall to the energy and passion of youth.

Tom Outland, the prototypical American (in character, much like Jay Gatsby of F. Scott Fitzgerald's novel, published in the same year as *The Professor's House*), is the landscape made manifest. His story is literally suspended between the two sections that describe Godfrey's crisis. Tom is word and flesh and place. Louie Marsellus participates in blurring the distinction between these entities by naming his home after his wife's former fiancé. For both St. Peter and Outland, places come to stand for the self.

Unlike nineteenth-century women writers for whom enclosed places represent painful confinement, St. Peter and Tom Outland are freed by enclosure and threatened by open space.[18] Tom Outland feels safe and protected in his cliff city dwelling, whereas Jim Burden is afraid of the vast, undulating terrain of the Nebraska prairie. Of course, Cather's safely enclosed characters must always have a vista. Every nurturing room must have a view.

In the second volume of *No Man's Land*, subtitled *Sexchanges*, which explains fundamental patterns in twentieth-century writers' work, Sandra Gilbert and Susan Gubar suggest that Cather values her literary foremothers who are able to "capture those moments of being before the emergence of an eroticism predicated upon the social constructions of gender."[19] Although some of the ways in which Gilbert and Gubar use this statement may not address the heart of Cather's concerns about human longing (one may question their faulting of Cather for what they perceive to be her fear of adult sexuality), one of Cather's strengths as a writer who chronicles human development is, as Gilbert and Gubar suggest, her ability to portray authentically those longings that both predate our ability to articulate them and survive regardless of our ostensible adulthood. And the desire to return to those spontaneous moments of pleasure in one's body (apart from logical consciousness) directs a number of important Cather's characters (Jim Burden, Godfrey St. Peter, Tom Outland) at a very primary level. In these moments of exhilaration for Tom in the mesa and for St. Peter in his attic room, one owns one's own body. And this freedom is vitally connected to place.

Tom Outland is interested in incommensurable space: "But the really splendid thing about our city, the thing that made it delightful to work there, and must have made it delightful to live there, was the setting. The town hung like a bird's nest in the cliff" (*PH* 213). Cather allows Tom to reside in the ideal place: suspended in air, like Marian Forrester in Niel's arms. Cather literally suspends Tom's story in the middle of the novel, and she suspends Tom's experiences in time and place. Perhaps no geographical location in all of Cather's fiction contains more unalloyed pleasure than Tom Outland's cliff city. Cather returns to this image at the beginning of *Death Comes for the Archbishop*. In her prologue, Cather situates the Roman Catholic clergymen in a landscape strongly reminiscent of Tom Outland's cliff city and Thea Kronborg's Panther Canyon: "The hidden garden in which the four men sat at table lay some twenty feet below the south end of this terrace, and was a mere shelf of rock, overhanging a steep declivity planted with vineyards."[20] Cather suggests, in both *The Professor's House* and *Death Comes for the Archbishop*, that important decisions get made in protected places with magestic vistas.

Like the shelf of rock in Rome, the place from which Latour's sufferings will start, the ruins of Tom Outland's cliff city contain powerful evidence of sorrow and suffering (as exemplied by Mother Eve). Yet even though the excavations cause Henry's death, Tom and Roddy, suspended in their cliff city, apart from civilization and in the ruin of an ordered civilization, are in a perfect place between rock and sky. When Tom is on the mesa he thinks, "Once again I had that glorious feeling that I never had anywhere else, the feeling of being *on the mesa*, in a world above the world" (*PH* 240). Protected from weather but exposed to the air "that tasted so pure" (*PH* 200), he is in truly mythic geography: a land of consciousness and comfort.

In her early story, "The Enchanted Bluff," the mesa represents an unattainable aspiration, ever far off, because of the vicissitudes of life in community. But in Tom Outland's story, the cliff city is a realizable dream, no less vital, poignant, and gripping because it has been reached. In *The Professor's House*, true mystery achieved remains mysterious. In *The Song of the Lark*, Thea Kronborg discovers what it takes to be an artist as a result of her time in Panther Canyon. She uncovers the deepest sources of art: fidelity, stamina, and silence. The eroticized landscape facilitates both her artistic and sexual awakening: the sun "bored into the wet, dark underbrush. The dripping cherry bushes, the pale aspens, and the frosty *piñons* were glittering and trembling, swimming in liquid gold."[21] Fred Ottenburg recognizes Thea's identity in relation to landscape. He feels she possesses "a personality that carried across big spaces and expanded among big things."[22] In Cather's first extended consideration of the cliff cities, the landscape distinctly separates a female character from domesticity. In "Writing Against Silences: Female Adolescent Development in the Novels of Willa Cather," Susan Rosowski describes Thea's coming of age: "within a crack in the earth and within a cave, Thea Kronborg learns about her potential to serve as a receptacle. She takes nothing tangible from the canyon, not trinkets or artifacts; instead, she leaves with the realization that she has inherited a female legacy to make a 'vessel' of herself."[23]

Conversely, Tom Outland wishes to make a home with Roddy in the cliff city. He domesticates space and gives it meaning by civilizing it. Cather suggests that we create ourselves out of the land. The inhabitants of the cliff city " 'built themselves into this mesa and humanized it'" (*PH* 221). They give meaning to their landscape, and it, in turn, defines them. Father Duchene gives words to describe the power of the cliff city: " 'Wherever humanity has made the hardest of all starts and lifted itself out of mere brutality, is a sacred spot'" (*PH* 221). The builders of the cliff city live suspended between their summer life on the plains and their winter life in the cliff city, hidden and protected. They are in Cather's idealized place. As a result of the lessons he learns from Tom Outland and his mesa, Professor St. Peter realizes that he needs his study, suspended above the world with his "ideal" forms.

James Woodress reminds us that Cather "wrote in the front of a presentation copy [of *The Professor's House*] to Robert Frost that 'This is really a story of "letting go with the heart." ' "[24] For Cather, this novel is, at least in part, about the way in which, at a moment of severe crises, one must let go of the excess baggage in one's life to enact the fundamental process of self-definition. Godfrey must be willing to live suspended between the demands of his family and the life of the mind he wishes to maintain for himself. He must learn the lesson of Tom Outland's tenure in the cliff city. He must make a home for himself, suspended from the demands of family life.

For Cather, this process very consciously involves a recognition of those relationships between individual and landscape (as in Tom Outland's desire for a suspension in "an ocean of clear air" [*PH* 213] that his Blue Mesa allows him); between individual and architectural structure (as in Professor St. Peter's attachment to the familiarity and comfort of the attic room); and between individuals (as in the intimate relationship between St. Peter and Tom Outland). In *The Professor's House*, the self-defining recognition always involves an understanding that the deepest connections often exist outside of conventional relationships, and in spaces of necessary separation and isolation.

In this novel, community means greed. Jealousy directs every character at one time or another. The work is suffused with characters who desire to possess. Properly, no one ought to own Tom Outland, but everyone does have a personal stake in either his body, his work, his legacy, or his life energy. Perhaps Cather directs our judgment of those who wish to possess Outland and all he stands for when Professor St. Peter and his daughter Kathleen discuss Rosamond and Louie's usurpation of the Outland name and money. Kathleen fondly remembers Tom's stories, which were freely given to the St. Peter girls as love gifts. She says, " 'Our Tom is much nicer than theirs'" (*PH* 132). Here Cather indicates that even the most apparently appealing characters wish to possess a version of Outland for reasons of self-preservation. Tom's companionship provides a way for Godfrey St. Peter to recapture his own lost youthful exuberance and to feel a deep and abiding kinship with another soul. The editing of Tom's journal offers the professor a way to retell Tom's story in a manner that is part Tom and part Godfrey. Perhaps it is best to say mostly Godfrey. Tom Outland's diary is very much a "thing not named" in Cather's fiction: a text that is both absent and present.

Cather's characters here don't grow up in our conventional understanding of the process. They undercut our associations of maturity defined as final responsibility to others. Godfrey has already experienced years of familial duty, and, in part because his family no longer needs his energy in the same way it once did, to develop fully, he must move toward a letting go of his family, his profession, and even his memory of Tom Outland. He must make the leap to radical *dispossession*.

Many critics suggest that St. Peter experiences a malaise of middle age, which renders him powerless, helpless, and paralyzed. For instance, Susan Rosowski asserts that "Cather was profoundly sensitive to feelings we term modern: a sense of alienation and historical discontinuity, of schism between the individual and the world, of joylessness."[25] St. Peter is also intellectually active in his apparent passivity, much like the female heroes of fairy tales, who must go through a period of sleep (like St. Peter's near-death experience) to reawaken, or be metaphorically kissed awake by a nurturing Augusta, to a new understanding finally of what one can possess: one's own life.

Perhaps Cather's genius lies in her recognition that this deep taking stock of what one can possess or understand of the self rarely happens before middle age—until one sees where one has been and then wonders what is left to conquer. Unlike Rosamond and Louie, who wish to find "just the right sort of hinge and latch" (*PH* 39) for their mock-Norwegian manor house, Professor St. Peter wishes to find his very self, his very life.

In her depiction of St. Peter's lecture to his students, a talk whose intensity Godfrey's wife Lillian considers "in rather bad taste" (*PH* 70), Cather uses St. Peter as her mouthpiece to express again her theory of what remains consistently interesting to human beings. As Cather has suggested before, no great work can be created without desire, for "Desire is creation, is the magical element in that process" (*PH* 29).

In his lecture, Godfrey articulates a key issue regarding inhabiting an alternate landscape. In speaking of the artists whose work attempts to account for the presence of God in human actions, St. Peter says, "They might, without sacrilege, have changed the prayer a little and said, *"Thy will be done in art, as it is in heaven.* How can it be done anywhere else *as* it is in heaven?"* (*PH* 69). Here Cather anticipates the allegorical mode she will adopt more fully in her next two novels. In many ways in *The Professor's House*, Cather is experimenting with the issues of worship and of doubleness of place that she will later develop in *Death Comes for the Archbishop* and in *Shadows on the Rock*. In his lecture, Godfrey, an academic, raises the question of the split between the flesh and the spirit that Latour solves, at least momentarily, through his worship and meditation at the beginning of *Death Comes for the Archbishop*. Lost in a maze of canonical hills, Latour finds the cruciform tree.[26] He suspends himself between the demands of his physical state and the place of abandonment reached by the contemplative: "Empowered by long training, the young priest blotted himself out of his own consciousness and meditated upon the anguish of his Lord. The Passion of Jesus became for him the only reality; the need of his own body was but a part of that conception."[27] Latour performs God's will on earth, as it will be done in heaven. He overcomes the limitations of a physical landscape by imagining a beloved, if painful, place.

Speaking for Cather (who was certainly not a simple modern, for she did not place her ultimate faith in the scientific method), St. Peter also asserts that " 'Science hasn't given us any new amazements'" (*PH* 68) and that " 'Art and religion (they are the same thing, in the end, of course) have given man the only happiness he has ever had'" (*PH* 69). St. Peter also describes the importance of mystery. Ritual must acknowledge the value of daily activity. St. Peter contends that Christian theologians (like great artists) get " 'splendid effects by excision'" (*PH* 69):

> They reset the stage with more space and mystery, throwing all the light upon a few sins of great dramatic value—only seven, you remember, and of those only three that are perpetually enthralling. (*PH* 69)

For Cather, in *The Professor's House* especially, of pride, covetousness, lust, anger, gluttony, envy, and sloth; finally, anger, covetousness, and envy remain those sins of consistent interest. *The Professor's House* is fundamentally about the destructive quality of envy: Kathleen and Scott McGregor are all but paralyzed by its force. Professor St. Peter must avoid the danger of that kind of self-destruction. He ultimately creates his own, internal, acceptable Tom Outland, one he can possess with freedom because his Outland has nothing to do with social contracts or material possessions.

Any valuable possession must ultimately involve self-possession. Any radical growth must be interior. And in *The Professor's House*, that growth is intrically connected to landscape. In a 1949 foreword to *Willa Cather on Writing*, Stephen Tennant suggests that "Willa Cather's art is essentially one of gazing beyond the immediate scene to a timeless sky or a timeless room."[28]

Judith Fryer has elaborated on that assertion and has used Bachelard's work in *The Poetics of Space* to provide an interesting explanation by which to understand St. Peter's movement through the novel. In *The Professor's House*, the mystery surrounding possession of geographical and architectural space is a representation of the desire to capture what Bachelard calls intimate immensity:

Immensity is within ourselves. It is attached to a sort of expansion of being that life curbs and caution arrests, but which starts again when we are alone. As soon as we become motionless, we are elsewhere; we are dreaming in a world that is immense.[29]

Tom Outland's Blue Mesa and Professor St. Peter's attic room allow these men the intimate immensity necessary for them to take possession of their own lives.

Cather's genius lies in her understanding that the Professor is correct in moving away from his family. This novel is about how people fail to communicate or to understand human experience when they presume that partners continue to need each other in the same way they once did. In his near-death experience, St. Peter learns a new way to exist in relationship to his family. The Professor thinks of Euripides: "'[W]hen he was an old man, he went and lived in a cave by the sea, and it was thought queer, at the time. It seems that houses had become insupportable to him'" (*PH* 156). St. Peter can face the future because he has found himself through the isolated places he has inhabited.

At fifty-two, Cather's age when she published the novel, St. Peter begins to understand his grandfather's behavior in old age. He thinks about himself and wonders if "he might be quite as near the end of his road as his grandfather had been in those days" (266). Godfrey wants "to run away from everything he had intensely cared for" (275). While Godfrey both stays and runs away at the end of *The Professor's House*, Cather would, in the six years after she published this work, write three novels about exile, about people who must both "let go with the heart" and hold tightly to the landscapes most dear to them.

4

My Mortal Enemy:
Willa Cather's Ballad of Exile

I

At the end of *The Professor's House*, Godfrey St. Peter consciously lets go of his family ties. He intends to live truly
suspended from the demands of relational life. He creates a
place for himself that is much like Tom Outland's mesa: separated from contemporary human interaction. In her next
novel, a work Marcus Klein describes as in its "form the most
severe and in its implications the most furious" of her
novels,[1] Cather explores the darkest results of the step to
break away from family connection. If *The Professor's House*
is about how to live in self-imposed emotional exile, and
Death Comes for the Archbishop and *Shadows on the Rock* are
about how to live in fruitful exile, *My Mortal Enemy* is about
how to die in exile. Myra Henshawe experiences several difficult exiles in her passionate life, yet it is interesting to note
that the novel begins with a picture of Myra *returning* to
Parthia after years of self-imposed exile.

While James Woodress acknowledges the darkness inherent in the vision presented in Cather's briefest and most
intense work, he also acknowledges the novel's power: "It is
a complete entity and an almost perfect work of art."[2] In
"Miss Jewett," an essay about Sarah Orne Jewett, Cather's
friend and mentor, in *Not under Forty*, Cather describes the
power of fine stories:

Walter Pater said that every truly great drama must, in the end, linger in the reader's mind as a sort of ballad. One might say that every fine story must leave in the mind of the sensitive reader an intangible residuum of pleasure; a cadence, a quality of voice that is exclusively the writer's own, individual, unique. A quality which one can remember without the volume at hand, can experience over and over again in the mind but can never absolutely define, as one can experience a memory or a melody, or the summer perfume of a garden.[3]

Cather is after the anatomy of exile in *My Mortal Enemy*, and, as in the ballad form, every detail contributes to that effect.

My Mortal Enemy represents the bitter apotheosis of the issues of exile Cather worked on all of her life. In his introduction to the novel, Klein reminds us of Cather's adolescent friendships: "Her companions in the village were the old men and women, anyone whose real life had been elsewhere."[4] Cather's early experience of her immigrant neighbors in Red Cloud, Nebraska, immersed her in the anatomy of exile and gave her the themes she would continue to work out in *My Mortal Enemy* and her other novels about the life of those separated from the rich associations found in their native lands.

Her later experience of returning to Red Cloud as an adult and a successful novelist might have contributed to the *form* Cather chose for this novel. In the twenties, when Cather was visiting home, she tried to live a simple life with her family. She did not often visit outside of the Cather family home, and she spent many peaceful hours with her parents: "In the evenings the family usually listened to Victrola records, which Cather had sent from New York, some of them made by her operatic friends Fremstad and Farrar. Her parents, however, preferred songs of their native South, spirituals, and popular nineteenth-century ballads."[5] To be at home without the demands of sociability involved listening to the powerful narratives found in popular ballads.

Although many of Cather's fictions include the experience of exile, in no other novel is this condition presented more starkly than in *My Mortal Enemy*. In a conversation with Alexandra Bergson in *O Pioneers!*, Carl Linstrum says, "there are only two or three human stories, and they go on repeating themselves as fiercely as if they had never happened before; like the larks in this country, that have been singing the same five notes over for thousands of years."[6] Although Carl's statement represents a foreshadowing of the brutal violence that will befall Marie and Emil (a violence that grows inexorably from intense passion) and a look forward to the title of Cather's next novel, Carl could certainly be speaking of the story of exile that suffuses Cather's fiction.

II

During a time when I was thinking seriously about *My Mortal Enemy*, a friend came to my house to practice some English folk ballads before she had to perform them in public. As she played the guitar and sang moving versions of "Barbara Allan" and "The Unquiet Grave," I realized how Cather's novel embodies the haunting (almost eerie), bittersweet, mournful, and passionate attitude toward human longing and love present in the songs I was listening to.

In *My Mortal Enemy*, Cather presents a ballad of exile, a complex narrative of love and loss whose haunting resonances suggest more than meets the eye. The novel contains moments of intense longing and passion, which correspond to the stanzas of a popular ballad. In *The Ballad Tradition*, Gordon Hall Gerould defines the ballad form:

> The Ballad ... wherever we find it, is concentrated; the action is so massed that we do not get the effect of a skeletonized long story, but of a unified short story, complete in itself, not infrequently implying events before and after but always fairly well centred on a single main event.[7]

The main event in *My Mortal Enemy* is the banishment of Myra Driscoll into permanent exile; this moment determines all subsequent action in the novel. Of course, this is not the first event we hear of. Cather chooses to begin her novel years later, during Myra's return from banishment. Interestingly, in our first look at her, Myra is "seated upon the sofa and softly playing on Cousin Bert's guitar."[8] Just as in *Death*

Comes for the Archbishop, Latour is both the suffering Jesus of the stations of the cross and the faithful Christian participating in the practice, so Myra, in *My Mortal Enemy*, is both the object of the ballad and the balladier.[9]

In a letter, Cather explains that in this novel "she was painting a portrait of Myra with reflections of her in various looking glasses."[10] With this description of her technique, Cather places herself firmly in the modernist tradition. As in a cubist painting, different forms (or geometrical shapes in a painting) must be put together by the audience or viewer to create a human figure. The reader of *My Mortal Enemy* must piece together an acceptable Myra from the various looking-glass reflections.

In *The Popular Ballad*, Francis B. Gummere describes the very basis of ballad: "The point is that incremental repetition is the fundamental fact of ballad structure."[11] Just as the conventional ballad form provides key refrains that set and reinforce mood, tone, and theme, so *My Mortal Enemy* presents no less than ten key physical and emotional experiences of exile. Every major character, Myra, Oswald, Nellie, Lydia, John Driscoll, must undergo at least one significant exile. Each must learn to live banished from a beloved place.

A simple list of the experiences of exile in the novel suggests that Cather creates a world of bitter people who must learn to live and die alone. Myra Driscoll Henshawe is an orphan who recreates that pattern in her adult life. She is an involuntary orphan as a child and then a deliberate orphan when she abandons her uncle's house. John Driscoll himself leaves Parthia as a young man to make "his fortune employing contract labour in the Missouri swamps" (*MME* 11–12). He then returns to display his wealth to his kinsmen.

Oswald Henshawe exiles himself from Parthia to New York long enough to make enough money to marry Myra. Even though Oswald is the literal exile, Myra feels banished from his presence and affection. She recounts her feelings of isolation to Nellie many years later: " 'I've not forgotten; those hot southern Illinois nights, when Oswald was in New York, and I had no word from him except through Liddy, and I used to lie on the floor all night and listen to the express trains go by' " (*MME* 87). This image of the deserted lover longing for an absent beloved is a standard ballad subject, clearly seen in "Scarborough Fair" and "Lord Lovel." The experience of passionate longing for an absent lover is particularly evident in the sixth stanza of the folk ballad, "The Seeds of Love":

> The willow tree will twist,
> And the willow tree will twine;
> I oftentimes have wished I were in that young man's arms
> That once had the heart of mine.[12]

Myra's sexual and emotional frustration—her separation from the beloved terrain of passion and approval—leads her to choose deliberate separation from her uncle's affection and his fortune.

Cather provides Myra's mirror image in Nellie Birdseye, who must also experience first an exile from the Henshawe apartment in New York, then a literal exile to a "sprawling, overgrown West-coast city" (*MME* 57), where she re-encounters Oswald and Myra. She is also an emotional exile from the immature, romantic conception of the Henshawe elopement she had harbored as an adolescent.

During her final illness, Myra bolts her door, a self-imposed exile from Nellie's intrusive presence. Like the religious women who now reside at her uncle's home, which has been converted into a convent, during her sickness Myra is, as Oswald says to Nellie, in self-imposed "retreat" (*MME* 77).

Near the end of the novel, Myra again repeats the experience of exile. Just as she had run away with Oswald to marry, so now in her mortal malaise, she secretly leaves her home to elope with death. Myra makes a sacrament of her voluntary exile to her cliff. She seeks meaning through her presence there. Myra is interested in what theologian Sandra Schneiders calls "the sacramentality of place which is at one and the same time earthy and material yet transcendent of matter."[13] Myra dies as she has lived, in exile and fundamentally alone. Cather uses topography to suggest Myra's isolation.

My Mortal Enemy, Cather's bitterest vision of human relationships, presents an orphan who longs for love. Beneath

Myra Henshawe's bitter laughter and sardonic humor lies a desire for connection. She, like Bartley Alexander, believes she can exist in only one place. She must choose between her uncle, who represents financial security, and her lover Oswald, who provides admiration and passion. Myra chooses romantic love, to her lifelong regret.

Perhaps nowhere in Cather's *oeuvre* are place and self more painfully and beautifully linked. Cather's words in praise of Tolstoi's fiction could serve to describe her own use of the details of place in her fiction, especially in *My Mortal Enemy*. Cather suggests that Tolstoi's interiors "are always so much a part of the emotions of the people that they are perfectly synthesized; they seem to exist, not so much in the author's mind, as in the emotional penumbra of the characters themselves."[14] Of all Cather's heroines, perhaps Myra Henshawe is most fully defined by the interiors she calls her own.

In her description of Nellie's first glimpse of Myra's New York apartment, Cather sexualizes the environment. The rich decor encodes Nellie's desire for Myra: "The long heavy velvet curtains and the velvet chairs were a wonderful plum-colour, like ripe fruit. The curtains were lined with that rich cream-colour that lies under the blue skin of ripe figs" (*MME* 26–27). Myra is the object of Nellie's fascinated affection, and the rooms the older woman creates suggest the power of her control over the impressionable girl.

Myra attempts always to exert control over her environment. When angry at life's bitter realities, she poisons the space she inhabits, yet she is capable of transforming her domestic spaces into warm, inviting spaces or into evil, dangerous locations. Returning to an important image from *The Professor's House*, Cather describes Nellie Birdseye's intense emotional reaction to Myra's anger toward Oswald after their argument about the mysterious key. When she hears the bitter words Myra speaks to Oswald, Nellie thinks, "I was afraid to look or speak or move. Everything about me seemed evil. When kindness has left people, even for a few moments, we become afraid of them. When it has left a place where we have always found it, it is like shipwreck; we drop from security into something malevolent and bottomless" (*MME* 51). The presence of anger in the once-enchanted apartment on Madison Square changes the complexion of the entire environment. After their argument, Myra again behaves as she always does when threatened: she exiles herself, this time from Oswald. She quickly arranges a journey to visit friends in Pittsburgh.

Like Bartley Alexander, Myra refuses to live suspended between two places. She has burned her emotional bridges behind her. She can't go back; she won't go back. Her relationship with Oswald has undermined the possiblity of suspension between beloved places. In his paraphrase of an unsual letter Cather wrote to an aspiring writer, James Woodress provides Cather's description of Myra: "It was the extravagance of her devotions that made her in the end feel that Oswald was her mortal enemy, that he had somehow been the enemy of her soul's peace. Her soul, of course, could never have been at peace. She wasn't that kind of woman."[15] This passage is reminiscent of the refrain in *Alexander's Bridge*, "It's like the song; peace is where I am not" (*AB* 70–71). Myra and Bartley Alexander long for an alternate landscape that will reconcile longing for stability and the appeal of passion.

Because she can't live suspended between a beloved memory and her current reality, Myra tries to poison even Oswald's memories of youthful pleasure: "He's a sentimentalist, always was; he can look back on the best of those days when we were young and loved each other, and make himself believe it was all like that. It wasn't" (*MME* 88). She becomes angriest when Nellie suggests letting up on Oswald. Myra is, in many ways, her uncle's niece. Both Driscolls are able to find another's weakness and use it to inflict pain. John Driscoll uses Myra's pride against her, as Myra constantly reminds Oswald of his professional inadequacies.

Driscoll leaves a stipulation in his will that Myra is to be received into the home he endows for destitute women in Chicago, and that she is to be "kept without charge, and paid an allowance of ten dollars a week for pocket money until the time of her death" (*MME* 81). John Driscoll forsees his postmortem triumph and revenge for Myra's disobedience. Once poor, Myra is therefore in the worst kind of situation Cather can imagine. She "can't take the road at all" (*MME* 65). If the road is all (as Cather firmly indicates in "Old Mrs. Harris" when Mr. Rosen quotes Michelet to Vickie Templeton:

"'*Le but n'est rien; le chemin, c'est tout.*' That means: The end is nothing, the road is all"),[16] then Myra's immobility is truly terrible.

Much critical interest has rested in the definition of Myra's mortal enemy. Critics have suggested it could represent Oswald, Nellie, Myra herself, old age, illness, death. Cather herself defined Oswald as the mortal enemy: "At the time the book came out, she wrote her old friend George Seibel: 'I had a premonition you would understand [that it was Oswald]— and that most people wouldn't.'"[17] For me, Myra's mortal enemy is the need to choose between two places. The fact that she must decide between economic security and romantic love is insupportable to her. Because she has chosen Oswald, she has had to forsake the Driscoll fortune. At her death, Myra is alone with the need for choice and alone with the choices she has made. The mortal enemy that pervades Cather's fiction is the recognition that any human choice, of lover, of home, of vocation, involves a rejection of alternate choices (and alternate landscapes), which could have provided pleasure and fulfilled desire.

At the end of the novel, Oswald exiles himself to Alaska. There he scatters Myra's ashes. The major characters in the novel look for places unpolluted by bitter memories. Oswald finally adopts Myra's method of managing pain. While Myra has been most interested in creating a "place in the world" (*MME* 75) for herself, the resolution of the novel pictures her eternally displaced or exiled from all she has known.

This novel represents Cather's darkest vision of human choice, her bitter ballad of exile. In *My Mortal Enemy*, Cather provides a series experiences of exile that serve as stanzas punctuated with a frightening refrain. Nellie reminds us of the haunting ballad refrain a the very end of the novel:

> Sometimes, when I have watched the bright beginning of a love story, when I have seen a common feeling exalted into beauty by the imagination, generosity, and the flaming courage of youth, I have heard again that strange complaint breathed by a dying woman into the stillness of night, like a confessional of the soul: "Why must I die like this, alone with my mortal enemy!" (*MME* 104 –5)

Cather's use of the evocative power of the ballad form allows the play of human emotions to take center stage. In her essay, "The Novel Demeuble," Cather suggests the desirability of the technique of reduction and simplification:

> How wonderful it would be if we could throw all the furniture out of the window; and along with it, all the meaningless reiterations concerning physical sensations, all the tiresome old patterns, and leave the room as bare as the stage of a Greek theatre, or as that house into which the glory of the Pentecost descended; leave the scene bare for the play of emotions, great and little— for the nursery tale, not less than the tragedy, is killed by tasteless amplitude. The elder Dumas enunciated a great principle when he said that to make a drama, a man needed one passion, and four walls.[18]

In *My Mortal Enemy*, Cather presents fundamental human passions reduced to a powerful narrative of loss and love.

Even so, Cather also gives Myra the answer for the restless exile, who must always search for the inviolate place. Myra says to Father Fay, "Religion is different from everything else; *because in religion seeking is finding*" (*MME* 94). Cather's next two novels present pilgrims who, like Myra, must come to terms with the dilemma of exile. James Woodress describes the circumstances of the novel's composition: "It belongs to the same dark mood that possessed Cather as she and her professor worked themselves through their mid-life crises. It is the most bitter piece of fiction she ever wrote, the most tragic, and it drained the last bit of gall from her system."[19] Willa Cather's most pessimistic artistic vision describes death in exile, while from her hard-won optimism come two novels, *Death Comes for the Archbishop* and *Shadows on the Rock*, which describe characters who find ways to learn to live in exile.

5

Death Comes for the Archbishop:
"L'invitation du voyage!":
The Search for the Sacred Place

> Purity does not lie in separation from but
> in deeper penetration into the universe.[1]
> —Teilhard de Chardin

> An empty place is a place of potential.[2]
> —Laurie Anderson

> There are passages in the life of every one
> which are too sacred for public gaze, and
> the making of them known can be justified
> only by extraordinary reasons.[3]
> —Machebeuf

I

Willa Cather felt that she had extraordinary reasons for using Reverend Machebeuf's sacred moments. Through the life stories of two French missionary priests, Cather is able to describe the search for the sacred place, to explain fidelity to a beloved landscape (for those living in exile), and to embody the need to be suspended between at least two landscapes simultaneously. In Machebeuf's story, she had found a narrative about voluntary exiles that combined movement and pause. Here she takes the raw materials of the missionary priests' lives and transforms them into a story about landscape and access to the sacred.

62

In the summer of 1925, Willa Cather "came across a rather rare book, *The Life of the Right Reverend Joseph P. Machebeuf*, by a priest named William Howlett."[4] Edith Lewis indicates that this reading was transformational for Cather: "In a single evening, as she often said, the idea of *Death Comes for the Archbishop* came to her, essentially as she afterwards wrote it."[5] A comparison between Howlett's biography and the novel reveals Cather's profound dependence on this work for her characterizations of the two priests (particularly Vaillant), her major events, her pervasive themes, and her major symbols. Susan Rosowski suggests that coming to terms with Machebeuf's story by tranforming it into her own narrative allowed Cather "to discard the dualism that had become debilitating and to celebrate literature in a new key—that of symbolism."[6]

When Willa Cather visited her brother Douglass in Arizona in 1912, she found "a whole new landscape—not only a physical landscape, but a landscape of the mind, peopled with wonderful imaginings."[7] Cather would first use this landscape in *The Song of the Lark* as the background against which Thea Kronborg experiences the sacredness of her self, apart from her family and her professional aspirations. Not until she found the Howlett biography was Cather able to imagine a story that could combine landscape and sacramentality. Rosowski makes clear the power of Roman Catholic worship and practice for Cather; in it she discovered "the most important single idea she took from Catholicism— divine love or *agape*. With it, she found in religion the means to continue her lifelong commitment to vindicate imaginative thought in a world threatened by materialism."[8]

The vital importance of place so suffuses *Death Comes for the Archbishop* that it is impossible to think of the novel without considering the places Latour and Vaillant inhabit, the places to which they travel, and the places they leave behind. As her best fiction indicates, Cather's imagination is drawn to stories that embody what Hélène Cixous has called the "marriage of a people with its land."[9] Elizabeth Hampsten suggests that "Cather has invested topography with an idea, and then adjusted character to it."[10] In fact, Cather, a writer with a geographical imagination, has very carefully chosen all of her stories so that character and topography are so intimately linked that no radical adjustment is necessary.

In Machebeuf's story, Cather found a narrative in which the truths presented "confound understanding in historical time."[11] To make the story of missionary priests her own, she had to follow what Rosowski calls "not a mimetic but an allegorical mode."[12] This way of seeing was particularly pleasing and natural to Cather, as Bernice Slote points out in her introduction to *The Kingdom of Art*: "From the beginning, as if by inheritance, Willa Cather absorbed the Bible and *Pilgrim's Progress*. Their presence in her writing is constant, insistent, and pervasive. Indeed, they made allegory familiar and natural to her, so that she *thought* allegorically (or symbolically), as these early critical pieces make very clear."[13] Slote suggests that early in her writing career, Cather developed "a style of mingled allusiveness and symbolism over a groundwork of fixed, related metaphors."[14]

It is easy to understand why Howlett's biography captured Cather's creative imagination. Machebeuf's is a story of fidelity and exile, of endurance and passion. In it, Cather found her new novel: "The biography was full of information about the lives and works of the missionary priests in the Southwest, documented by letters written by Father Machebeuf to his sister in France."[15]

In a letter of 14 February 1840, from Tiffin, Ohio, Machebeuf makes a request of his sister: "In my last letter I forgot to ask for at least two sets of the Stations of the Cross—one as large and fine as possible, for the new and beautiful church at Lower Sandusky which we are going to begin building in the spring, and the other such as it may be; it is for another little chapel now nearly finished."[16]

Cather writes a novel in which the tension between movement and stasis is manifested in the opposition between the Stations of the Cross and devotion to Mary. There are no fewer than thirty explicit references to Mary, the mother of Jesus, in the novel. Two of these references, Juan Diego's miracle and Vaillant's "The Month of Mary," are extended meditations on the power and significance of that symbol. The priests undertake seventeen long journeys in the course of the novel. Although the stations are not mentioned as a specific devotion in the novel itself, the emphasis on the faith journey the two missionary priests enact suggests that Cather chose to use the references to the stations from the Howlett biography as a controlling metaphor for Latour and Vaillant's life of pilgrimage. In these two forms of piety, Cather finds two ways to worship, one that emphasizes movement and doubleness of space, the other quiet contemplation.

The stations were first introduced for the faithful who could not be literal pilgrims in the Crusades, so they enacted the pilgrimage in their churches and in their own souls. In making the stations of the cross, one enters a literal landscape in the church itself and an ideal landscape in which the pilgrim worshiper removes herself to the location of Christ's suffering and death. A note in the Howlett biography explains that the "Stations (or Way) of the Cross are a set of fourteen episodes from the passion, death, and burial of Jesus for devotional consideration. The practice of following the Way of the Cross began in Europe when the faithful were prevented from going on pilgrimage to the Holy Land, and by the sixteenth century common practice had settled on the present fourteen events."[17] The stations suggest movement and stasis (both rest in action and action in rest): "*rest in action* was his hope of life."[18] Machebeuf's, and, by extension, Vaillant's, dedication to Mary (pervasive in the Howlett biography) and his practice of the Stations of the Cross as a form of devotion pervade Cather's work.

Death Comes for the Archbishop is Willa Cather's reach into the geography of hope. There exists a tension between the missionary journeys Latour and Vaillant undertake and the possibility of home (of redemption and salvation) they experience. For every torturous journey of faith, there is a scene of rest and succor.

In her perceptive essay describing Cather's narrative structures, "*Death Comes for the Archbishop:* Cather's Mystery and Manners," Merrill Maguire Skaggs explains that "Latour's life contains as many trials as a cathedral contains stations of the cross."[19] For Skaggs, Latour's life, the cathedral he builds, and the novel itself must be understood as parallel constructions whose component parts meld and merge in Cather's grand design.

To dramatize the tension between movement and stasis, Cather presents another Roman Catholic devotion. The stations represent both pilgrimage and stasis simultaneously. They are journey, and they are rest. The stations are embodied in the novel not only through the trials Latour undergoes. There is also a careful shifting of emphasis from one character to another in relation to the stations. Latour is not merely the Christ of the journey through suffering and death. Cather interestingly alters the focus of the stations. Yes, the reader must, by sharing the priest's story, follow the road of the cross with Latour, yet Cather does more than allow Latour to stand for the suffering Christ. Latour and the reader must pause at key moments and reflect on events. At times Latour is the suffering servant (the Jesus of the stations); at others he is the figure who provides sustenance to his beleaguered friends, as when he ministers to the sick Vaillant; and at other times he represents the performer of the stations, who must reflect on another's suffering. Certainly, Cather begins her novel with a prologue that condemns Latour to a journey of suffering and redemption, but it is Cather's genius to erase the distinctions among the suffering servant, the providers of aid, and the performers of the devotion. Cather's characters, and her readers alike, are carefully enmeshed in a structure that inextricably links them in a common journey of discovery.

Clinton Keeler suggests Cather's emphasis on movement and stasis when he describes her use of the frescoes of the life of Ste. Genevieve by Puvis de Chavannes, which Cather said determined the style of the novel. In his analysis of the novel's Prologue, Keeler describes the technique Cather adopts, in part, from that nineteenth-century French artist: "the suggestion of intense feeling is framed by stillness."[20] Indeed Cather's whole novel can be said to contain restless movement framed by a calming stillness. Cather describes anxious exiles who turn their anxiety into architecture, into belief.

Of course, Latour and Vaillant have very different personalities, very different needs, as embodied by the two different kinds of structural symbols associated with them. Latour's life and the cathedral he commissions become as one, whereas Vaillant's character is symbolized by the rough but sturdy wagon constructed for his journey to the new diocese in Colorado.

A comparison with the visual arts may help explain the dichotomy of movement and pause in *Death Comes for the Archbishop*. Helen Frankenthaler's two works, *Natural Answer* (1976) and *Into the West* (1977), were inspired by the landscape of the southwest. The catalog for a recent Museum of Modern Art exhibition of her work could be describing Cather's fictional techniques: "These works mark another shift in her oeuvre, toward a more complex, illusionistic composition, with greater atmospheric qualities."[21] *Natural Answer*, composed in 1976, suggests restless movement. The whites overlaid on the terra cotta hues indicate one sphere of action occurring simultaneously with another. Even Frankenthaler's description of the composition of the piece suggests anxious motion: "I worked long and hard on it— going to and from it I must have walked miles."[22]

In her 1977 work, *Into the West*, the same colors are used to suggest pause, rest, and peace. The process of composition of this work is remarkable in its similarity to Cather's techniques in *Death Comes for the Archbishop*: "But unlike *Natural Answer*, which is a complex additive composition, *Into the West* emerged out of a series of subtractions."[23] One thinks of the elements of narrative technique Cather chose to ignore in her narrative. *Death Comes for the Archbishop* is not primarily about plot (although the patterns of her character's actions are vitally important); it is about mood and atmosphere. For Frankenthaler, *Into the West*, which suggests profound periods of pause, of rest, of home, of rightness, was the more difficult piece to accomplish: "Every millimeter of that huge surface had to have 'perfect' color placement yet look as if it all occurred in a flash."[24]

In *Death Comes for the Archbishop*, restless movement is constantly juxtaposed with periods of peaceful reflection. At moments of greatest stress, Cather's characters turn to the Mother of God.

Cather began to consider the role of Mary while working on *The Professor's House*. In a scene that occurs on Christmas day, Professor St. Peter and Augusta discuss the power of

Mary's story. St. Peter (a stand-in for Cather in this instance) is woefully ignorant of the devotion to Mary, but he finds Augusta's faith provocative. This scene may help to explain the puzzling "forms" that inhabit St. Peter's attic study. Mary, who in *Death Comes for the Archbishop* represents the very image of patient faith, is, in the Christmas scene in *The Professor's House*, connected to the forms in his attic. When speaking of the dressmaker's dummies immediately after his chat about the Virgin Mary with Augusta, St. Peter thinks of Augusta's faith, "Sometimes she made those terrible women entirely plausible" (*PH* 101). Cather's language suggests that the Professor is referring to both the forms and to Mary.

In *Death Comes for the Archbishop*, Cather, like Augusta, makes the value of Mary entirely plausible. It is clear that Cather was very much concerned with the forms of mother-hood in *The Professor's House*. St. Peter refuses to let go of the dressmaker's forms, even as he acknowleges that he must let go of everything else, and Tom Outland is fascinated by Mother Eve, the mummy he finds in the cliff dwellings. Father Duchene even calls her "our lady" (*PH* 223) at one point.

The Howlett biography explains that when Machebeuf was taught by his own mother, she stressed "that tender devotion to the Mother of God which clung to him during his whole life."[25] His own beloved mother died when he was thirteen. His sister wrote years later, " 'his grief would have been without solace were it not for his devotion to the divine Mother.' "[26] For Machebeuf, the paradox of rest in action and action in rest is embodied in the Magnificat in the first chapter of Luke. Machebeuf worked untiringly in his seminary years, writing and rewriting sermons he would use throughout his life, and "a large portion of these sermons had the Blessed Virgin for their subject."[27] The novel asks and answers the question: Why does Vaillant, like Machebeuf, so need the figure of the patient and protective mother?

Three times in the novel the key scene of Vaillant's painful vacillation at the moment of leaving his father's house is repeated. The young priest is terribly afraid of leaving his place of birth. The novel is about voluntary exiles, orphans who must learn to live in the alternate landscape. Cather here is interested in what Elizabeth Shepley Sergeant has called the "fateful rending that grips at the exile's heart."[28] For Latour and Vaillant, the exile's life is made endurable by devotion to Mary, the figure of gentle protection.

The novel stands as an examination of the need to alternate between rest in a beloved place, which nourishes and refreshes the spirit, and productive movement. Through her description of two missionary priests, Cather finds a way to tell a story about how to reconcile movement and pause. Latour and Vaillant must live within the paradox of religious life that demands action *and* contemplation. Cather's description of landscape reinforces the doubleness of place and the need to exist in two landscapes simultaneously.

The first pages of *Death Comes for the Archbishop* directly connect the powerful landscape of *The Professor's House* with the story of Roman Catholic missionaries in the New World. The description of the landscape of late afternoon Rome at the beginning of *Death Comes for the Archbishop* is a direct reflection of Tom Outland's cliff cities. For those in exile, the Old World and the New become intermingled, indistinct. Later in the novel, Cather says of Latour, "in the Old World he found himself homesick for the New."[29] The description of the landscape suggests a suspension between the ancient world of the American Southwest and the center of Roman Catholic worship. The scene serves as an invitation to pilgrimage for the reader, who must remember the sacred landscape of *The Professor's House* and think forward to the terrain of New Mexico.

The three Cardinals and the missionary Bishop sit together in a "hidden garden" (*DC* 3), which is "a mere shelf of rock" (*DC* 3). At the heart of the Old World there exists a mirror image of the most ancient and sacred place in the New World. The distinction between old and new loses its clarity. Like the intense blue air of Tom Outland's mesa, the shelf of rock in Rome is surrounded by "the drop into the air" (*DC* 3). Here the prelates are suspended between heaven and earth while deciding the fate of Jean Marie Latour. Rome itself resembles Latour's Santa Fe: "The low profile of the city barely fretted the skyline—indistinct except for the dome of St. Peter's" (*DC* 4). This image prefigures the city Latour will create in his New Mexican diocese, where the cathedral he commissions stands as the landmark for all pilgrims.

The prologue to the novel sets up the important themes, tensions, images, and associations with place. A question remains for the reader: What happens to the El Greco mentioned in the prologue? Maria de Allande has a selfish interest in Latour. He hopes to recover a valuable painting once begged from his family by a shrewd Franciscan missionary. We learn that it is a "St. Francis, of almost feminine beauty" (*DC* 12).

While the painting itself is never recovered, Cather does provide a closely related image that indicates that Latour is a man of refinement and taste, humanity and insight. Magdalena, rescued from the evil Buck Scales, is transformed by the efforts of Latour and Vaillant, as well as by the Sisters of Loretto. She becomes the living St. Francis:

> She advanced in a whirlwind of gleaming wings, and Tranquilino dropped his spade and stood watching her. At one moment the whole flock of doves caught the light in such a way that they all became invisible at once, dissolved in light and disappeared as salt dissolves in water. The next moment they flashed around, black and silver against the sun. They settled upon Magdalena's arms and shoulders, ate from her hand. When she put a crust of bread between her lips, two doves hung in the air before her face, stirring their wings and pecking at the morsel. (*DC* 209–10)

Latour is able to transform human beings into living saints. His work of art is not only represented by the cathedral, but also by the lives he rescues—the lives that enrich his own. Latour does not rescue the lost El Greco, but he is able to rescue Magdalena from horrible Buck Scales. The description of the mature Magdalena reinforces her connection with the lost El Greco. As an adult she possesses "the deep claret colour under the golden brown of her cheeks" (*DC* 210). The browns and surprising claret, along with his signature greens and grays, suggest the El Greco palette.

When the reader first encounters Father Latour, he is surrounded by a horrifying landscape of similarity. Traveling in a cubist nightmare, Latour is a modernist Ethan Brand, surrounded by ovenlike hillocks as far as the eye can see and horse can travel. Unlike Ethan Brand, Latour does not search to find the unpardonable sin; he must look for grace. Like Brand, Latour will die as a result of his search, but Cather's vision is much gentler than Hawthorne's. Latour must learn to journey and to rest; he must reconcile movement and stasis.

Death Comes for the Archbishop is a series of juxtapositions between pilgrimage, and places of pause and rest. The novel is a compendium of important places. Latour and Vaillant define themselves in relation to place. Latour is happier with making "homes": places of rest for himself and those he cares for. Vaillant is more comfortable on the move. Vaillant has few faults because he is able to reconcile these two ways of being. He finds comfort wherever he is. Vaillant is the true contemplative, who reconciles thought and action, and who is able to find the love of God wherever he goes.

Latour and Vaillant must acknowledge and therefore transform secular spaces into shrines. These missionary priests find physical locations that suggest powerful theological mysteries. Places come to represent endurance, stamina, fidelity, and immanence. Here Susan Rosowski's ideas on allegory are particularly useful: "In *Death Comes for the Archbishop* Cather wrote of a highly developed power of symbolization which provides meaning to the most ordinary acts and the most disparate objects."[30] In her description of landscape, Cather is using an allegorical mode in that the "effect is of a magical world in which correspondences link heaven and earth, past and present, history and legend."[31] Because it is an important means through which they can acknowledge the sacred, Latour and Vaillant must be willing to recognize the miracle present in landscape itself. In discussing miracle, Latour suggests that in moments when the grace of God overtakes us, "our eyes can see and our ears can hear what is there about us always" (*DC* 50). His words to describe miracle could well speak for landscape, which provides access to the holy.

The term "pilgrim imagination" suggests Cather's way of seeing. She recognizes the constancy of journey. Even as her characters pause for rest, they know they must remain on a journey because in Cather's fiction "seeking is finding."

Peace pervades the landscape and the human heart when the function and the experience of a physical place merge. When the tormented Sada escapes her "owners" and takes sanctuary in the doorway of the sacristy, Latour measures his own lack of faith against the power of Sada's belief. Like Latour, Sada must accommodate absence and exile from the sacred place: he "knew that his poverty was as bleak as hers" (*DC* 218). Her Protestant owners harbor a bigoted fear of Roman Catholic practice, and Latour is advised that it would be politically unwise to force them to let Sada worship as she wishes. So Latour tells Sada that he will pray for her always, and he gives her "a little silver medal, with a figure of the Virgin" (*DC* 218). The medal is an invitation to pilgrimage for Sada. Like Latour's prayer at the beginning of the novel, the medal will transport Sada at any time from a place of misery and exile to a sacred place of worship.

The dense scene serves to reveal Cather's major concerns in the novel. After his encounter with Sada, Latour experiences a moment of perfect pause: "The peace without seemed all one with the peace in his own soul" (*DC* 219). This scene of recognition in exile serves as a dramatic contrast to Bartley Alexander's repeated refrain: peace is where I am not. In Cather's universe, one experiences peace, connection with the surrounding world, when one accepts the condition of exile and finds ways to transform that state into meaningful worship. At his moment of tremendous peace, when Latour makes profound connection with another wretched exile, Cather's description of landscape reinforces the doubleness of space: "the gauzy clouds that had ribbed the arch of heaven were now all sunk into one soft white fog bank over the Sangre de Christo mountains" (*DC* 219). Heaven and earth merge in the soft fog (which will play a similar role for Cécile Auclair in *Shadows on the Rock*) over the mountain range that reminds the people of another sacred moment: the Savior's suffering and death. Cather reminds us that the moments of peace are rare and brief. She presents us with an image of motion, represented by a footprint left behind, which will also figure prominently in her later novel, *Lucy Gayheart*. After Sada leaves, Latour stands "in the doorway of his church, lost in thought, looking at the line of black footprints his departing visitor had left in the wet scurf of snow" (*DC* 219). In *Death Comes for the Archbishop*, moments of peace are ephemeral and are followed immediately by the demands of movement.

Another key moment of rest occurs when Latour finds *Agua Secreta*. Here the priest interrupts his restless journey and sleeps in a soft bed, after anticipating "a dry camp in the wilderness" (*DC* 29). In this place of pause and rest, Latour "lay in comfort and safety, with love for his fellow creatures flowing like peace about his heart" (29). Latour must learn to balance action and rest in his place of exile.

II

"Tonight we are exiles, happy ones, thinking of home." (*DC* 36)

Death Comes to the Archbishop presents a picture of the need to live with a recognition of doubleness of space. Cather provides not fewer than ten moments when her characters exist in one landscape and remember the sweet demands of another. The novel represents Cather's intense interest in the imagination in exile.

One of the most powerful invitations to pilgrimage comes in the form of the vestments created by the nuns at Vaillant's sister's, Mother Philomène's, convent. When Latour visits the convent, one of the younger sisters tells him of the pleasure they take in letters from the New World:

how precious to them were Father Vaillant's long letters, letters in which he told his sister of the country, the Indians, the pious Mexican women, the Spanish martyrs of old. These letters, she said, Mother Philomène read aloud in the evening. The nun took Father Latour to a window that jutted out and looked up the narrow street to where the well turned at an angle, cutting off further view. "Look," she said, "after the Mother has read us one of those letters from her brother, I come and stand in this alcove and look up our little street with its one lamp, and just beyond the turn there, is New Mexico; all that he had written us of those red deserts and blue mountains, the great plains and the herds of bison, and the canyons more profound than our deepest mountain gorges. I can feel I am there, my heart beats faster, and it seems but a moment until the retiring-bell cuts short my dreams." (*DC* 181–82)

Father Vaillant's letters to the Sisters in France reflect Cather's own technique in the novel. Like Cather's work, Vaillant's letters give the land a profound voice, which speaks even to those who have never literally seen it. Cather's novel adds to the Machebeuf biography by showing directly how an alternate landscape can come alive for an appreciative reader. The nuns in the act of making vestments for the missionary priests are transported to an alternate landscape of depth and beauty, which enriches their lives.

The story of Father Joseph's painful vacillation at the thought of leaving his home to study for the priesthood is repeated at several key moments in the novel. It is the last scene Latour remembers as death comes for him. Jean Latour's brave exclamation to his friend Joseph can stand as a controlling refrain for the novel. As the *diligence* rumbles down the road, Latour makes his final plea: "'Allons!' said Jean lightly. 'L'invitation du voyage!'" (*DC* 285). The novel depicts a series of invitations to voyage for all its main characters. Those with whom we feel deepest sympathy and connection accept the invitation to live in two landscapes simultaneously.

On one Christmas Day, Latour and Vaillant share a countryman's dinner in which they reminisce about home. Joseph does his best to create a meal appropriate to the occasion. Latour, a man of taste and refinement, recognizes the value of the meal he is eating. He finds doubleness even in his soup, which he suggests "is not the work of one man. It is the result of a constantly refined tradition. There are nearly a thousand years of history in this soup" (*DC* 39). Like the horn of the *diligence*, the soup is an invitation to pilgrimage, which asks the Frenchmen to remember and savor their traditions of home while in the New World.

Because their meal has readied the men for reminiscence, over the dessert of dried plums "they fell to talking of the great yellow ones that grew in the old Latour garden at home. Their thoughts met in that tilted cobble street, winding down a hill, with the uneven garden walls and tall horse-chestnuts on either side; a lonely street after nightfall, with soft street lamps shaped like lanterns at the darkest turnings" (*DC* 41– 42). The lonely street they both remember suggests the exile's loneliness on the holiday evening. The plums are another invitation to pilgrimage, like Proust's madeleines, which transport the sensitive soul back to a place of beloved memory. Although Cather calls these reflections "an indulgence they [the priests] seldom permitted themselves" (*DC* 42), the novel is suffused with meditations of this kind. The busy missionary priests may feel they have little time for memories of home, yet Cather is vitally interested in those moments.

On a missionary journey, as Latour approaches the clean pueblo of Isleta, his spirits rise. He sees the acacia trees that awaken "pleasant memories, recalling a garden in the south of France where he used to visit young cousins" (*DC* 85). In the landscape of the American Southwest, Latour can be suddenly transported back to the geography of childhood. Cather is interested in sacred moments when Latour and Vaillant must live suspended between two landscapes at once. As Rosowski notes, the "effect is of a magical world in which correspondences link heaven and earth, past and present, history and legend."[32] This allegorical mode allows Cather to represent past, present, and future simultaneously.

Near the end of the novel, Cather provides a vivid description of the kind of journeying between the landscapes of past and present that human beings perform within their own consciousness. As Latour prepares to accept death when it comes,

> He observed also that there was no longer any perspective in his memories. He remembered his winters with his cousins on the Mediterranean when he was a little boy, his student days in the Holy City, as clearly as he remembered the arrival of M. Molny and the building of his cathedral. He was soon to have done with calendared time, and it already ceased to count for him. He sat in the middle of his own consciousness; none of his former states of mind were lost or outgrown. They were all within reach of his hand, and all comprehensible. (*DC* 290)

On one level, this is an accurate description of the ways the mind changes as a person ages. Often memories from long ago supplant more recent experiences. But Cather also gives us an important key to her technique in the novel. Just as she asserts that the frescoes of Ste. Genevieve by Puvis de Chavannes suggested her way of proceeding, so Latour's lack of perspective is very important to her ideas in the novel. In the frescoes, all action, major or minor, occurs on the same plane. Cather's consideration of memory indicates that past landscapes are as valuable as those presently before us.

The answer for Cather's restless exiles is never a final return to the beloved landscape of memory. For Latour, that would only mean the need for yet another alternate landscape. In *Death Comes for the Archbishop*, Cather continues to describe the quest for the inviolate place, that place which reconciles the literal landscape and the sacred place of memory. Of course God is always the creator of that interior space, but Latour and Vaillant find a reflection of that place in the glory of God's creation. As a result of miracle, they see (and Cather allows us a glimpse) in the physical world a shadowy reflection of interior, spiritual landscape.

Cather is drawn to Roman Catholic practice and theology because the celebration of the Eucharist itself is the primary place in which the literal act and the sacred place are reconciled. The cathedral is the inviolate place where the two landscapes meet. Dutch theologian Henri Nouwen provides a beautiful description of the doubleness of time and space as it is manifested in the celebration of the Eucharist: "The Lord is at the center of all things and yet in such a quiet, unobtrusive, elusive way. He lives with us, even physically, but not in the same physical way that other elements are present to us. This transcendent physical presence is what characterizes the Eucharist. It is already the other world present in this one. In the celebration of the Eucharist we are given an enclave in our world of space and time. God in Christ is really here, and yet his physical presence is not characterized by the same limitations of space and time that we now know."[33]

Cather finds in the experience of Latour and Vaillant an example of the quest for the sacred place or sacred moment that allows for the use of the language of Christian worship. In the rituals of missionary work and in the building of the cathedral, Cather finds a symbol system and a physical embodiment of the desire to make space sacred. Landscape itself represents relation to God. The Eucharist is meal and word: It is an incommensurable place of rest to approach with awe. Here Cather mixes the drama of the land with the drama of worship.

III

Teilhard de Chardin has written, "Purity does not lie in separation from but in deeper penetration into the universe."[34] Latour must accomplish this deeper penetration to fulfill his dream of building the cathedral and to receive grace.

In the literal and spiritual center of the novel is a section, entitled "Stone Lips," in which Latour and Jacinto are caught in a blizzard and must take shelter in a remote and sacred cave. This moment combines many of the aspects of space and place that Cather has been using in the novel. The scene represents a major rite of passage for Latour. The image combines pause (Jacinto and Latour must interrupt their important journey) and movement (Latour must move to a new recognition of the depth and complexity of Jacinto's fidelity).

Even though the two must stop, the movement of the earth's deep river is apparent to Latour. He feels a distrust for the coldness and vibration of the place, yet he still hopes to explore the cave more fully when Jacinto is asleep. When Latour awakens, Jacinto is standing with his arms stretched out, against the sacred opening in the wall of the cave. Like the cathedral, the cave stands as a sacred place, dedicated to transcendence and connection.

Latour knows he is in the presence of forces that are powerful and ancient: the snake, the river, the fire. Like Shelley's Prometheus, Latour encounters a daemonic power. He hears the spirit's utterance. That powerful, transfixing voice stays with him and helps him recognize the need to build his cathedral. He is in clearly mythic geography, a holy place, a place of creation where he perceives life at its most elemental.

Jacinto is a picture of Cather, his ear available to the fundamental energy of the earth. Through the agency of Jacinto and his time in his guide's cave, Latour finds a way to understand passion, yearning, fruitfulness, and worship.

Cather is interested in places that lead her characters to a recognition of the movement of the sacred in the world. A sacred place in Willa Cather's fiction is a spot in which an individual recognizes connection with the transcendent. The quest for the sacred place provides what historian of religion Belden Lane calls the "turn of focus that brings the holy into view."[35] In Cather's fiction, a character reaches a sacred place when both points of the suspension between beloved places are merged and reconciled. That never happens for Bartley Alexander, who goes under with his cantilever bridge, but it does occur several times for Bishop Latour, particularly in Jacinto's cave.

Mircea Eliade calls the cave "a break in the homogeneity of space."[36] He suggests that this "break is symbolized by an opening by which passage from one cosmic region to another is made possible (from heaven to earth and vice versa; from earth to the underworld)."[37] At this most profound place of connection, Latour must pause and surrender his control. He must come face to face with physical presence, with the roaring of waters and the fetid smell of the cave.

Jacinto's cave must be read allegorically. "Being an *axis mundi*, the sacred city or temple is regarded as the meeting point of heaven, earth, and hell":[38] The images surrounding cave experiences in *Death Comes for the Archbishop* and *The Song of the Lark* suggest fear of chaos, the threat of loss of control, and finally a way to integrate the disturbing oppositions that could destroy the self. The cave is sexual: vaginal, anal, oral. It is the location in which one must face the self, in which one must reconcile outside and inside, self and other. Latour cannot build his cathedral unless he experiences his own horror in Jacinto's cave. The bishop must experience difference before he can envision the place of profound connection. Latour's time in the cave is his descent into the underworld, and he does return with a boon for himself and for his people. Cather's parable of Jacinto's cave is a way to understand the need to accommodate the demands of a culture and worship system other than one's own. The retreat into the cave is a literal pause in his journey, and it suggests Latour's need to come to terms with profound human questions about the nature of worship.

Any sacred place represents the struggle against death: "the rock of the Temple in Jerusalem reached deep into the *tehom*,"[39] which "symbolized the chaos of waters . . . and, at the same time, the world of death."[40] Latour is on a pilgrimage whose end is death and life.

Throughout the novel the bishop encounters shrines and antishrines, places of comfort and locations of remarkable violence. He must constantly be on pilgrimage and then return. His cyclical pilgrimages force him to separate and return with frightening regularity. After his experiences in the cave, Latour returns to "virgin snow" (*DC* 132), to a more radical innocence that will allow him to build his cathedral.

Cather shows her command of classical and Christian references in her scene concerning Vaillant's description of another important cave. Near Tuscon, a Pima Indian shows Vaillant a "golden chalice, vestments and cruets, all the paraphernalia for celebrating Mass" (*DC* 207) hidden within the depths of a cave. Vaillant says, "To me, that is the situation in a parable" (*DC* 207). By situation he means the circumstance of the unconverted native population: the "lost Catholics" (*DC* 206). But with this image of the secrets of the cave, Cather suggests something important about how we use images. Cather presents a parable of the cave in which human life is a mere reflection, simply a shadow of the fuller world we miss within our earthly existence. Cather combines classical and Christian ideas of absolutes. The religious articles stored in the cave allegorically suggest the glory of transubstantiation, and of immanence. As images, they hold tremendous power for their people.

IV

The human end in the spirit's greatest reach,
The extreme of the known in the presence of the
extreme of the unknown.[41]
—Wallace Stevens
"To an Old Philosopher in Rome"

In the last section of *Death Comes for the Archbishop*, Cather is after the geography of eternity, as is Wallace Stevens in "To an

Old Philosopher in Rome," which owes much of its tone and content to Cather's novel. In a letter written in 1940, Stevens says of Cather, "we have nothing better than she is. She takes so much pains to conceal her sophistication that it is easy to miss her quality."[42] Like Stevens's philosopher's reveries, Latour's thoughts become like frescoes, without perspective.

Even the spot Latour chooses for his "period of reflection" (*DC* 265) on retirement suggests a return to a beloved landscape and a preparation for death. Early in his career, as he rides to the Tesuque mission, he finds "a little Mexican house and a garden shaded by an apricot tree of such great size as he had never seen before" (*DC* 266). Latour believes that "the heat of the sun, reflected from the rocky hill-slope up into the tree, gave the fruit an even temperature, warmth from two sides, such as brings the wall peaches to perfection in France" (*DC* 266). For his retirement retreat, where he prepares for death, Latour chooses a spot that suggests the ripeness of his beloved homeland. Latour urges his new priests to create orchards: "Wherever there was a French priest, there should be a garden of fruit trees and vegetables and flowers" (*DC* 267).

The Cathedral itself suggests France in the New World. While it is made from the stone of a local mountain, it is Midi Romanesque, as one would see in France. It is both organic, of the region, and foreign, from Latour's native land.

As the Archbishop realizes that he will soon die, he speaks "only French to those about him" (*DC* 269). He relaxes his long-standing rule to speak only in English or Spanish while in his mission. With the change of his long-held rules, he begins his journey back to his origins.

In Willa Cather's fiction, identity is often connected with landscape. Self cannot be understood apart from place. Near the end of his life, Latour looks on "the Cathedral that had taken Father Vaillant's place in his life after that remarkable man went away" (*DC* 271). The building of the structure, the creation of the perfect product, can, for Cather, act as a substitute for a missing loved one. When Father Latour returns to Santa Fe after his fever, he loves the "nearness to his Cathedral" (*DC* 273). Latour craves "the open, golden face of his Cathedral" (*DC* 271).

Even the Sangre de Christo mountains suggest a double-ness. The sight of the mountains suggests "the colour of the dried blood of saints and martyrs preserved in old churches in Rome, which liquefies upon occasion" (*DC* 273). Topography itself takes one back in time and place.

The answer for the exile in Cather's fiction is not a return to the beloved place, but the maintenance of that beloved place in sweet memory. When in Clermont (the place Latour's associates assume he will return to in his old age), "his heart lay like a stone in his breast. There was too much past, perhaps" (*DC* 274). Neither point of the cantilever, past or present, is sufficient. One must remain suspended between the literal landscape and the beloved "mythic geography." "He did not know just when it became necessary to him, but he had come back to die in exile for the sake of it" (*DC* 275–76): Latour lives a life dedicated to learning to live in exile. The condition becomes so familiar that he is finally unable to return home. Unlike Myra Henshawe's experience of dying, during which she fights against the demands of the community that surrounds her, Latour's death in exile is a triumph in which physical space and the sacred place are reconciled within the self through prayer.

At the end of *Death Comes*, as Latour nears his own death, he remembers "his own misguided friend, Kit Carson" (*DC* 293), who follows the Navajo people until they make their stand at Canyon de Chelly, which remains "an inviolate place, the very heart and centre of their life" (*DC* 293). In the American southwest of *Death Comes for the Archbishop*, the sacred center of one's life is always embodied as a physical place. Cather juxtaposes the sacred places of the Native American population and of Roman Catholic missionary exiles.

The last book of the novel is Cather's meditation on transformations of consciousness and the quest for the sacred space. It represents a compendium of Cather's issues and techniques. In that final section, Cather presents two stories of Holy Families, both inextricably connected to place. Father Junípero finds the Holy Family on his arduous journey across desert wastes. The land *itself* is family to the Navajos: "That canyon and the Shiprock were like kind parents to his people, places more sacred to them than churches, more sacred than any place is to the white man" (*DC* 295).

Father Junípero's narration of his miraculous encounter with the Holy Family perfectly encapsulates Cather's descriptions of journey and rest. Junípero, like Latour, experiences the horrors of the desert journey, and he benefits from the aid of the Holy Family. The story makes a great impression on Bishop Latour: "He had such affection for that story, indeed, that he had allowed himself to repeat it on but two occasions" (*DC* 282). Surely the Bishop here is Cather's substitute. Like Latour, Cather has told two stories of Holy Families, one Christian and one Navajo.

A student assigned to read *Death Comes for the Archbishop* in a course, entitled "Religion and the Quest for Meaning in Life," chose to do her research paper on architecture and its relationship to worship. After learning about the construction of St. Francis Cathedral in Santa Fe she said, "As much as I try to imagine the church the archbishop builds, when I read the novel, I can't stop myself from thinking about my own parish church." This story suggests Cather's power of evocation. A reader finds her own life reflected in Cather's powerful images. She participates in the doubleness of association with the places that Cather creates. The actual landscape in Santa Fe, the fictional cathedral, and the reader's own life experience merge. Readers are drawn to Cather because she presents a mythic geography that suggests the sacramental nature of place.

In *Shadows on the Rock*, Cather's fictional universe is still suffused with Roman Catholic feeling, yet the sacred place is no longer merely the cathedral. The whole city is transformed into the sacred place. Late seventeenth-century Quebec is a place of exile where the beloved landscape and the literal landscape are reconciled.

6
Shadows on the Rock:
The Imagination in Exile

Nearly twenty years after the publication of *Alexander's Bridge*, Cather returned in her fiction to the St. Lawrence to depict a universe in which exiles need to make a life in the Canadian wilderness. *Shadows on the Rock*, a novel about the inner life of the exile, opens with Euclide Auclair watching the last sails of *La Bonne Espérance*, a sight that signals the beginning of the bitter winter with no news from France and no new provisions.

In "Willa Cather's Female Landscapes," Susan Rosowski suggests that to "an exceptional degree, Cather worked through her life by the method of incremental repetition she used in her finest novels. Images, symbols, themes that appear in her early poems and stories reappear, transformed and expanded, in her subsequent works."[1] This quality is very apparent in Cather's use of space and place. *Shadows on the Rock* is the result of Cather's constantly refined ideas about the exile's fidelity to a beloved landscape.

In *Shadows on the Rock*, Cather populated late seventeenth-century Quebec with immigrants and exiles who must, to survive, recreate the mood and manners of their French homeland. Euclide and Cécile Auclair need to remain suspended between their nostalgia for France and the demands of the new Canada they are in the process of creating.

As she does in *The Professor's House* and *My Mortal Enemy*, Cather here creates interior spaces that reverberate with meaning for their inhabitants. The warm and inviting apothecary shop, home of Euclide and Cécile, is one of the symbolic centers of the novel. In the dark Canadian winter, these rooms stand for the Old World civilization left behind. The rooms are, in fact, arranged just as they were in France, according to the dying wishes of Cécile's mother: "She wanted to believe that when she herself was lying in this rude Canadian earth, life would go on almost unchanged in this room with its dear (and, to her, beautiful objects); that the proprieties would be observed, all the little shades of feeling which make the common fine."[2] This passage is reminiscent of Father Latour's discourse, in *Death Comes for the Archbishop*, on the French soup Vaillant creates in the American Southwest: "When one thinks of it, a soup like this is not the work of one man. It is the result of a constantly refined tradition. There are nearly a thousand years of history in this soup."[3] For Cather, civilization does not reside in the meta-narratives used to explain the course of history. Instead, a culture may be valued for the sweet rightness of the ordinary. Her novels stand as a reproach to those who define her as a nostalgic writer who refused to face the modern world. Cather's body of work is, in part, about characters who must accommodate dramatic change in their lives, who must create places, both figurative and literal, which may reveal the permanent in the midst of radical change.

In two works spanning Cather's most productive years as a novelist, we can see a concern with the demands of being suspended between two landscapes. Bartley Alexander dies, still torn by the bitter need for choice, whereas Euclide and Cécile Auclair help create a new nation because they realize they must inhabit both a literal landscape and a landscape of beloved memory.

In *Sapphira and the Slave Girl*, Cather's last published novel, Sapphira Dodderidge Colbert, Martin Colbert, Rachel Blake, and Nancy Till are all exiles who remember the demands of multiple landscapes. Cather writes a story of the declining culture of slave ownership to depict a universe full of exiles who are unsure of their proper place. Sapphira is exiled from her beloved Loudon County because of her déclassé marriage, and she lives by returning for renewal there. Even in her depiction of the doom and decay of a way of life, in *Sapphira and the Slave Girl* Cather creates characters who must be able to live in a state of suspension between families of origin and the homes individuals create for themselves. Unlike Myra Henshawe, who must renounce her inheritance, Sapphira is able to maintain connection in two places. Martin Colbert and Rachel Blake are exiled to a limited life on Back Creek, and Nancy Till is exiled from Back Creek.

Although Cather continues to describe the drama of exile even in her last novel, that state of being is worked out most forcefully in *Shadows on the Rock*. Here, much of character, action, and detail suggests that this is a novel about how to live in exile. Willa Cather had been working up to this task in all her previous novels. *Shadows on the Rock* combines the search for the sacred place with the demands of suspension and the notion of possession. Here she presents a compendium of ways to live in exile. It is important to note that no one is a completely willing exile. Even the sailors, who risk their lives on bitter ocean voyages, must return to their native lands for sustenance after long trips to and from Canada, and the inhabitants of Quebec advertise their wares with the dress of their native regions to remind the sailors of home.

Euclide Auclair survives in exile by recreating the details of the homeland as fully as possible. He creates order out of the chaos of the wilderness. One learns to thrive in exile by husbanding what is valuable so that it lasts until new supplies arrive. Euclide measures out his medicines throughout the long winter. When the ships from France return with Euclide's provisions, one "by one the white jars on the shelves, and the drawers of the cabinets, were filled up again; with powders, salts, gums, blue crystals, strong-smelling spices, bay leaves, lime flowers, camomile flowers, senna, hyssop, mustard, dried plants and roots in great variety" (*SR* 210). This list is a reminder that the least significant item takes on great value when it comes from home. Cather makes clear that the tiniest potion may restore one and that careful measuring is of great value.

But unlike *My Ántonia* and *A Lost Lady*, in which Cather chronicles young men's experience of exile, *Shadows on the Rock* is primarily interested in the female child's perception of the world of exile. Even though Cécile, because of her age, feels the burden of exile less forcefully than her father, she still must come to terms with its power. For Cecile, exile becomes home. Although she remembers France and wishes to maintain the decencies and habits of her native land, she perceives herself as a Canadian. Yet she is intrigued by the journey between France and Canada. "Cécile wondered how they could ever find it,—a goal so tiny, out of an approach so vast" (*SR* 208): Cécile's consideration of the difficulty of the transatlantic voyage is an image of the demands inherent in the search for the sacred place. Near the end of *Shadows on the Rock*, Willa Cather depicts Cécile Auclair's fascination with the dangerous and exciting voyage made by the tall-masted ships that finally reach Quebec. As Cécile gazes on *Les Deux Frères, Le Profond, La Reine du Nord, La Licorne*, and *Le Faucon* anchored safely in the harbor, she muses on the vast sea and the small harbor. This image of Cécile over-looking the harbor and her curiosity about the vessels' arrival is a snapshot of Cather's consideration of the quest for sacred place. The search is dangerous and threatening, yet the rewards of the effort are exhilarating. Cécile muses on the hardships endured by the faithful ships:

> They stood almost in a row, out in the river. Worn, battered old travellers they looked. It brought tears to the eyes to think of how faithful they were, and how much they had endured and overcome in the years they had been beating back and forth between Canada and the Old World. What adverse winds those sails had been trimmed to, what mountains of waves had beaten the sides of those old hulls, what a wilderness of hostile, never-resting water those bows had driven through! Beaten southward, beaten backward, out of their course for days and even weeks together; rolling helpless, with sails furled, water over them and under them,—but somehow wearing through. (*SR* 207–8)

This moving description can stand as an image of the work a pilgrim must undertake in the universe of Cather's novels.

Cather herself experienced the power of a transatlantic voyage while returning from Europe during the time she was composing *Shadows on the Rock*. Her journey on one of the

Empress liners brought her up the St. Lawrence to Quebec:
"The whole voyage became a sort of home-coming to *Shadows*, and the slow progress up the St. Lawrence, between
woods on fire with October, was its climax—a dream of
joy."[4] Cather translated her own experience of journey into a
novel of astounding beauty and richness.

The word "goal" appears another key time in the novel.
On Christmas eve, after a holiday dinner at the Auclair home,
the company starts for church services. As they reach the top
of the Rock of Quebec, they can see the parade of townspeople, restless pilgrims moving toward a church:

> Across the white ledges that sloped like a vast natural stairway
> down to the Cathedral, black groups were moving, families and
> friends in little flocks, all going toward the same goal,—the
> doors of the church, wide open and showing a ruddy vault in the
> blue darkness. (*SR* 113)

In Cather's late seventeenth-century Quebec, all are exiles
searching for the sacred place. The anthropomorphic (or,
more appropriately, gynemorphic) doors of the cathedral
invite cold wanderers into the warmth of connection. This
image suggests a reversal of the implications of Jacinto's
cave. Unlike Latour, who must force himself to inhabit the
sacred place of another culture, these pilgrims are drawn to
the portals of this inviting cave, which promises safety.

The novel begins with the settlement at its ostensibly
bleakest moment: the last sail of the final ship returning to
France is out of sight. *La Bonne Espérance* is gone. The
colonists must again live in wintertime Quebec. Euclide
Auclair stands on Cap Diamant, wondering how to survive in
exile, just as Cather is, at this time in her life, trying to imagine how to live without connection to home.

Sharon Daloz Parks's work on the metaphors that guide
faith development in men and women may serve as a theoretical foundation by which to understand how Cather's characters manage exile in *Shadows on the Rock*. Parks's essay,
"Home and Pilgrimage: Companion Metaphors for Personal
and Social Transformation," helps us read a novel that follows
not only the cycle of the seasons but also the calendar of the

liturgical year. Cather's deliberate structure reinforces a recognition of doubleness of space in which the faithful Christian inhabits her own physical location and simultaneously remembers the lives of the saints as memorialized by the feasts of the Church. The liturgical year provides a meaning-laden structure for the exile. Theologian Henri Nouwen describes the value of the liturgical cycle as he experienced it in a Trappist monastery: "It seems as if I am being slowly lifted up from the gray, dull, somewhat monotonous secular time cycle into a very colorful, rich sequence of events in which solemnity and playfulness, joy and grief, seriousness and lightness take each other's place on and off."[5] Nouwen's description corresponds to the ways Cécile experiences this cycle in *Shadows*. She uses the lives of the saints as a rich alternate world, full of passion and struggle, which both reflects her own deepest longings for connection and provides a stirring drama in which men and women seek the presence of God: that most sacred of places. The liturgical year helps Cécile shape and order her chaotic experience. It gives structure to this community of exiles.

To discuss the ways in which men and women must reconcile the opposing metaphors of faith development, Sharon Parks calls for a "renewed companionship of metaphors of detachment *and* connection, pilgrims *and* homemakers, journeying *and* homesteading."[6] This set of oppositions helps reveal Cather's (whose mind worked by acknowledging opposition) techniques in *Shadows on the Rock*. Parks suggests that the ideal reconciliation of these metaphors occurs "when this voice which expresses connection and relation comes to authentic speech" and it "joins the story of human development as a journey, pilgrimage, and adventure with a story of home, dwelling, and communion."[7] This intimate connection between pilgrimage and homesteading helps elucidate Cather's technique in *Shadows on the Rock*. The novel is a complex consideration of these companion metaphors in which character, event, and setting reinforce the abiding power of that opposition. Not surprisingly, Cather comes to some very interesting conclusions about this dichotomy.

Male and female characters in *Shadows on the Rock* subvert our conventional assumption that "Men tend to tell and to recognize their stories primarily in terms that celebrate moments of separation and differentiation. Women tend to tell and recognize their stories in terms of moments of attachment and relation."[8] Cather's characters, male and female, are both pilgrims *and* homemakers. The task of the exiled person is to live in precarious balance between these two ways of seeing. For every female homemaker, there exists a female pilgrim. Of course, Cécile Auclair is our most important pilgrim.

In "Archetypal Patterns in *Shadows on the Rock*," Susan Hallgarth charts Cecile's power as a Persephone figure who moves "from childhood to young maidenhood, a process of mother-daughter separation-and-reunion" through which she "discovers her own identity, transcends the limitations imposed by death, and symbolically represents immortality."[9] Hallgarth's reading emphasizes both Cecile's journey and her return home.

Cather subverts our conventional gender expectations of adult male and female behavior in her depiction of religious life in the novel. The Ursulines are willing pilgrims:

> When they came across the Atlantic, they brought their family with them, their kindred, their closest friends. In whatever little wooden vessel they had laboured across the sea, they carried all; they brought to Canada the Holy Family, the saints and martyrs, the glorious company of the Apostles, the heavenly host. (*SR* 96–97)

Cather clearly depicts these pilgrims respectfully; they are women able to live in precarious exile because they define what is valuable and keep it near them. The Sisters transcend exile and are "always cheerful, never lugubrious" (*SR* 97). They recognize the inevitability of doubleness of space. They know what it is to carry the sacred place within. This is the crux of Cather's play with space and place: Her characters must be willing to exist in at least two landscapes simultaneously—a landscape of beloved memory and a landscape of exile. Much of her fiction depicts this dilemma, but *Shadows on the Rock*, written in a period of deep loss for Cather, describes the profound need to balance the memory of beloved places with the demands of the present.

When Euclide and Cécile visit Mother Juschereau de Saint-Ignace to care for her sprained ankle, they find her making artificial flowers. She says, "These are wild roses, such as I used to gather when I was a child at Beauport" (*SR* 35). This image encapsulates Cather's technique of managing space in *Shadows on the Rock*. The Reverend Mother's exclamation is surely a reflection of Cather's remembrance of the wild flowers found on the prairie surrounding Red Cloud. The Sister uses handcraft to transport herself back to her native land. Like Frontenac's glass fruit, the artificial roses suggest the value of the fashioned artwork as a reminder of the doubleness of space. The nun's hobby reminds her both of home and of the Virgin Mary, for whom the rose stands as a symbol. The image also indicates that Cather never forgets anything. She has saved this image from the Howlett biography of Machebeuf, whose sister supplied him with artificial flowers for his treasured May altar in France.[10] In a novel that, at every turn, suggests the superiority of the artificial over the real, for the Reverend Mother, the flowers stand as a catalyst to pilgrimage back to the beloved landscape.

In *Shadows*, Cather presents without irony the following method of managing exile:

> When an adventurer carries his gods with him into a remote and savage country, the colony he founds will, from the beginning, have graces, traditions, riches of the mind and spirit. Its history will shine with bright incidents, slight, perhaps, but precious, as in life itself, where the great matters are often as worthless as astronomical distances, and the trifles dear as the heart's blood. (*SR* 98)

The rock of Quebec appeals to Cather as a setting for one of her most complex novels because the inhabitants refuse to renounce their native lands. Cather wrote to Governor Wilbur Cross of Connecticut, in response to his thoughtful review of the novel, about the appeal of this narrative: "These people brought a kind of French culture there and somehow kept it alive on that rock."[11] The French residents of Quebec define themselves as exiles, yet they keep France alive in the New World. The Ursuline Sisters are able to maintain a recognition of Christ's sacrifice as a living presence within their community, even while in exile from their native land. They are able to combine pilgrimage and home.

In *Shadows on the Rock*, Cather presents a male religious whose torment is in direct opposition to the Ursulines' peace of heart and mind. Noël Chabanel is a deeply reluctant pilgrim whose will to serve the souls in Canada results in "one long humiliation and disappointment" (*SR* 150). His inability to learn the Huron languages and his exquisite sensitivity to changes in food and climate render his life in exile a living torture. His greatest suffering derives from an inability to carry within himself a recognition of the sacred place. Father Hector describes Chabanel's

> Almost continual sense of the withdrawal of God. All missionaries have that anguish at times, but with Chabanel it was continual. For long months, for a whole winter, he would exist in the forest, every human sense outraged, and with no assurance of the nearness of God. In those seasons of despair he was constantly beset by temptation in the form of homesickness. He longed to leave the mission to priests who were better suited to its hardships, to return to France and teach the young, and to find again that peace of soul, that cleanliness and order, which made him the master of his mind and its powers. Everything that he had lost was awaiting him in France. (*SR* 152–53)

To overcome the temptation to return home, Chabanel makes a vow of "perpetual stability." The impulse to return to his native land is so great that nothing less than a sacred vow will keep him from fleeing. Unlike the Ursuline sisters, he seems unable to transport the personal security and comfort of home to his place of exile. For Cather, that limitation leads to downfall. The conflicted Chabanel dies soon after he makes his vow.

He seems a double for both the Ursuline Sisters and for Jeanne Le Ber (Cather's most extreme portrait of the pilgrim and homemaker in exile), who makes her family home a cloister and her bare cloister in the cathedral into a place of rest and security. Jeanne is a bad daughter but a good pilgrim, who combines physical stasis with a faith journey that is rich and redemptive for herself and Canada. In *Shadows on the Rock*, women seem far less reluctant pilgrims than men.

Cather presents restless male pilgrims, such as Bishop Laval in his fitful midnight walks through town (on one of which he finds abandoned Jacques and gives him the comfortable "home" he denies himself). Laval's early-morning ringing of the church bell to call the townspeople from their warm beds to a pilgrimage of faith to the sacred place where the Eucharist is celebrated also suggests the need to move from the present to a recognition of sacred events of the past. In *Shadows on the Rock*, Cather uses the bell, as she does in *Death Comes for the Archbishop*, as a catalyst, an invitation to pilgrimage through which fragile souls are encouraged to remember an alternate landscape.

At another key moment in the novel, Euclide and Frontenac share a moment of suspension between two places, brought on by the ringing of the bell:

> The Count fell into reflection, and his apothecary sat silent, waiting for his dismissal. Both were thinking of the scene outside the windows, under the low November sky—but the river was not the St. Lawrence. They were looking out on the Pont-Marie, and the hay-barges tied up at the Port-au-Foin. On an afternoon like this the boatmen would be covering the hay-bales with tarpaulins, Auclair was thinking, and about this time the bells always rang from the Célestins' and the church of Saint-Paul. (*SR* 250)

The landscape, the quality of light, and the bells of a church are able to transport a character to another time and place. Here the count and Euclide share a fantasy of home at the end of a day. The loving details of manual labor and the familiarity of a remembered routine are very moving to both men.

On All Soul's Day, the perfect moment to reconcile old and new, Bishop Laval rings the cathedral bell every hour: "It called out through the intense silence of streets where there were no vehicles to rumble, but only damp vapours from the river to make sound more intense and startling, to give it overtones and singular reverberations" (*SR* 94). Unlike the rumble of the *diligence*, which distracts Vaillant at his moment of great decision in *Death Comes for the Archbishop*, Quebec on All Soul's Day offers a welcome silence. These descriptions suggest the power of the bell's plea and its relation to the work of art. Cather's language for the sound of the bell could well be used in reference to her own art. Like the bell, the novel calls the reader to a recognition of loyalty to multiple landscapes. Cather's characters inhabit a universe of flesh and blood, but they remember the lives of those who have left this world in anticipation of the richer life to come. On All Soul's Day, loyalty is divided between the world of the living and the remembrance of the dead. This day reminds Cécile of the stories of Quebec: "All the miracles that had happened there, and the dreams that had been dreamed, came out of the fog; every spire, every ledge and pinnacle, took on the splendour of legend" (*SR* 95). The literal landscape becomes transformed. The bell calls Cécile to an alternate place of wonder and magic. In church on All Soul's Day, Cécile the homemaker becomes Cécile the pilgrim who travels to the sacred place of saints and martyrs.

Count Frontenac feels the power of the bell's summons when he experiences a fearful dream of his boyhood home and the giant who wishes to invade the beloved place of childhood protection. From within his dream, Frontenac responds to the churchbell's prodding. Laval's ringing wakens him from a dream of terror: "He knew that bell like a voice. He was, then, in Canada, in the Château on the rock of Kebec; the St. Lawrence must be flowing seaward beneath his windows" (*SR* 243). The sound calls Frontenac out of his revery, away from the beloved but threatened landscape of youth, back into his preparations to die. Frontenac must, as he says, "change my climate" (*SR* 248): take leave of this world.

Frontenac, torn between his love of home and his commitment to Canada, expresses a wish concerning his final resting place that suggests the tug between home and pilgrimage. He says to Euclide Auclair, "I shall be buried here, in the chapel of the Récollets, but I should like my heart to be sent back to France, in a box of lead or silver, and buried near my sister in Saint-Nicholas-des-Champs" (*SR* 249). Edith Lewis suggests the power this gesture held for Cather, who "visited . . . Saint-Nicholas-des-Champs, where Frontenac's heart was buried."[12]

The need for connection in the pilgrim landscape and in the native land suggests the deep truth that Sharon Parks articulates: "Our concepts of Spirit are inevitably linked to our yearning for transcendence, for crossing over, reaching beyond. We feel we are not *what* we ought to be, hence we are not *where* we ought to be."[13]

If we look to the experience of Cather's life as she was working on *Shadows on the Rock*, we recognize in the story of pilgrim exiles on the harsh rock of Quebec at the end of the seventeenth century a narrative through which she could explore ways to accommodate exile. This story naturally captured the artist's imagination.

Cécile Auclair makes her home in exile. The two states are reconciled for her, as they needed to be for Cather. When Count Frontenac considers returning home and Euclide Auclair naturally assumes he will follow his patron, Cécile is devastated. To return home, to the place of her birth, would deprive Cécile of all that she has made her own in Canada. At the time she was researching and writing *Shadows*, Cather herself was struggling with these serious issues of closeness and separation, of home and exile. On the evening of the first snowfall of the year as Cécile pulls Jacques up Holy Family Hill, she experiences a moment of being, which she describes as "this feeling of being in one's own place" (*SR* 104). Cather's life at the end of the 1920s allowed her only fleeting moments of this kind of pleasure. James Woodress describes the difficult decisions facing Cather as she wrote *Shadows*: "She had to give up the apartment she had lived in for fifteen years. It was a wrenching blow to leave the place she had loved and worked so well in for so long."[14] The drama of exile enacted in the novel was very close to Cather's experience in 1927–28: "At the peak of her career, a famous author, enjoying universal acclaim for her latest novel, she was a ship without moorings."[15] Her precarious position was soon to worsen.

Cather enjoyed a happy Christmas of 1927 with her family and didn't return to New York until late February. Her father (to whom she was very close) died one week after she left Red Cloud.[16] Of this death, Edith Lewis says, "It was a great shock to her—not only the personal loss, but her realization of the changes it foreshadowed."[17]   The changes included Cather's mother's stroke and partial paralysis (the dependence imposed by physical handicap always terrified Cather). Her trips to California to help care for her ailing mother were devastating to Cather. She wrote from California (which she detested) to a friend that working on *Shadows* "had been her only refuge."[18] Lewis suggests that the writing of *Shadows* was a way to remain in a universe of peace amid the catastrophe in her personal life: "It may have been in part a reluctance to leave that world of Catholic feeling and tradition in which she had lived so happily for so long [while writing *Death Comes for the Archbishop*] that led her to embark on this new novel."[19]

After Cather's mother's death, the family house in Red Cloud was no longer the focal point of Cather's experience of home. Lewis writes that after the death of Cather's mother and father, "the family as a family might almost be said not to exist any longer."[20] During this period of tragic upheaval in Cather's family of origin, she made five trips to Quebec.[21]

Near the end of *Shadows on the Rock*, Bishop Saint-Vallier speaks of inevitable change: "We are in the beginning of a new century, but periods do not always correspond with centuries. At home the old age is dying, but the new is still hidden" (*SR* 277).   These words could describe Cather's condition in 1928. With one parent dead and the other infirm, Cather was beginning a new age.

Shadows on the Rock represents the partially revealed new beginning. Lewis indicates that Cather rarely spoke of anything she intended to write. Even if she mentioned it, "she always left out its real theme, the secret treasure at its heart."[22] At the heart of *Shadows on the Rock* is a search for a place to call home and a presentation of models of how to live in exile. That is its secret treasure. *Shadows on the Rock* is a work that starts with loss and ends with joy. The composition and publication of this novel kept Cather going in one of the most difficult times in her adult life. Cather's friend Ferris Greenslet read the novel while in Quebec. He said that "No other book that I have read so completely recaptured the spirit of a place."[23] That place is both the literal city of Quebec

and the figurative place of exile, the space inhabited by the
orphan who must reconcile home and pilgrimage, who must
imitate the Ursuline Sisters and carry an experience of home
into exile. Like Count Frontenac, whose body remains in one
place and whose heart is in another, Cather's body is buried
in Jaffrey, New Hampshire, but her heart resides in the spaces
she makes sacred in her best fiction. James Woodress makes
a judgment with which it is easy to agree: "As a stylist and
impressionist in words, Cather never wrote anything better
than *Shadows on the Rock.*"[24]

Conclusion

> But the wooden foot-bridge over Back Creek hung just as it did
> the Colberts' time, a curious "suspension" bridge, without piles,
> swung from the far-reaching white limb of a great sycamore
> that grew on the bank and leaned over the stream.[1]

In the epilogue to *Sapphira and the Slave Girl*, Cather's last
published novel, Willa Cather finally uses the pronoun "I"
when she speaks from the perspective of a young girl, safe in
bed and waiting to meet Nancy Till, a black woman who had
been taken "across the river" (*SSG* 283) to escape from slav-
ery. The protected child anticipates the tale of exile and
return. This scene beautifully encapsulates Cather's ways of
dealing with character, narrative structure, and metaphors of
movement, landscape, as well as architectural and geographical space. This child inhabits the sacred place of the artist.
The scene is reminiscent of Thea Kronborg's experience of
sickness and comfort at the beginning of *The Song of the Lark*,
where she is wrapped in a protective cocoon by the nurturing
Dr. Archie. For Cather, this location represents the ideal
place of protection, the sacred place the adult artist must provide for herself. There is no more evocative state of being in
Cather's fiction than that of the enveloped consciousness
waiting for stimulation. The artist as a child must remain
suspended between the past she can only understand through
stories and the future in which she will tell those stories of
exile and return.

Even as Cather returns in her last published novel to a
description of her childhood home, she continues to describe

97

a doubleness in relation to place. Cather watches and learns from a woman who needs to cross over. Just as Myra Henshawe represents the person who is the subject "of the most interesting, indeed the only interesting" (*MME* 3) stories Nellie Birdseye knows, so when Nancy wishes to tell stories about the last days of the Colberts, the child "could almost have told her myself, I had heard about them so often" (*SSG* 291). Stories lodge themselves in our consciousness and will not let go.

Cather describes the privileged position—one's position in a place is always of vital importance to an understanding of character in her fiction—of the child who is wrapped in a blanket and carried to the window. The centrality of this child's vision is reinforced: The "actual scene of the meeting had been arranged for my benefit" (*SSG* 282). The world is ordered to accommodate her epiphany.

Nancy and Till "went on talking as if I were not there at all" (*SSG* 285). This is the primal scene for Willa Cather: to be in a listening posture, unnoticed, and undisturbed. Here, as is implicit in much of Cather's work, the female is the object of the female gaze. In *Playing in the Dark: Whiteness and the Literary Imagination*, a work about the ways in which race influences American writers, Toni Morrison reads *Sapphira and the Slave Girl* as a novel that offers "the compelling attraction of exploring the possibilities of one woman's absolute power over the body of another woman."[2]

The epilogue to *Sapphira and the Slave Girl* makes it clear that a writer must, as early as possible, blend with the place and become an unobtrusive part of the scenery. Cather's strongest characters are observers of others' secrets. This position allows those who are observed valuable narrative freedom: "Sometimes their talk was puzzling, but I soon learned that it was best never to interrupt with questions" (*SSG* 288).

Cather describes the tensions her characters often feel between inside and outside, between the desire for cosseting and for the wild, exhilarating weather outside: "I was something over five years old, and was kept in bed on that memorable day because I had a cold. . . . The slats of the green window shutters rattled, the limp cordage of the great willow trees in the yard was whipped and tossed furiously by the wind. It was the last day I would have chosen to stay indoors" (*SSG* 279). While the young child imagines the adventure is outside, she will soon learn that the story of another's adventure can be as exciting as one's own adventure. In *Sapphira and the Slave Girl*, the wilderness is inside.

Critics from Bernice Slote forward have acknowledged that Cather continued to rework themes present in her earliest writings: "principles of feeling, sincerity, the personal relationship, simplification, individuality; themes of the artist's untiring effort and devotion to his art, the loss of the woman in the artist, the beauty of language and the individuality of speech, the distance between the artist and the near-artist, the futility of reform; the interest in national character, the sense of the old world in the new; the importance of a 'good ear,' of subject matter found in human life, of both observation and sympathy."[3] In the final pages of Cather's last published novel, the reader is encouraged to understand that each reworking of material fulfills needs and provides valuable perspectives: Till's "stories about the Master and Mistress were never mere repetitions, but grew more and more into a complete picture of those two persons" (*SSG* 292). As Till retells the stories of her youth, Cather reworked her ideas about space and place throughout her career until they became a rich and compelling tapestry.

The genius of Willa Sibert Cather lies in her ability to turn a crushing blow into the very structural and metaphorical basis for her art. Cather's personal history of voluntary and involuntary exile helped her to understand the joys and agonies of a life of inevitable movement. Her characters' prevailing position is to be suspended between at least two places, needing a recognition of both to survive. Characters who cannot maintain this doubleness of association, such as Mr. Shimerda in *My Ántonia* and Claude Wheeler in *One of Ours*, are somehow punished for their failure.

A woman writer's strength has everything to do with her power to choose. That Willa Cather was deeply concerned about landscape, space, place, choice, and identity is a given. An artist inevitably reveals her own obsessions. The difference between the artist and the artist of genius is the willingness of the genius to do more than confront her obsessions. The genius explains them to her readers. Cather embodies the complexity of human choice by making clear the difficulties of the human experience. Cather is interested in paradoxical space, location that suggests doubleness: enclosed areas (rooms that suggest freedom) and wide vistas (prairies that threaten the integrity of the human spirit). She creates narratives in which physical locations come to stand for the interior lives of her characters, often restless exiles who must acknowledge the need for suspension between beloved terrains. Cather's descriptions of landscape help us to understand freedom, imprisonment, immanence, community, connection, isolation, integrity, authenticity, and incommensurability. Cather uses landscape to suggest possibility. She truly gives the land a voice.

Notes

Abbreviations

AB Willa Cather. *Alexander's Bridge*. Lincoln: University of Nebraska Press, 1977.

AL *Willa Cather. A Lost Lady*. New York: Vantage Books, 1972.

DC Willa Cather. *Death Comes for the Archbishop*. New York: Vintage Books, 1971.

MA Willa Cather. *My Ántonia*. Boston: Houghton Mifflin, 1954.

MME Willa Cather. *My Mortal Enemy*. New York: Vintage Books, 1954.

PH Willa Cather. *The Professor's House*. New York: Vintage Books, 1973.

SR Willa Cather. *Shadows on the Rock*. New York: Vintage Books, 1974.

SSG Willa Cather. *Sapphira and the Slave Girl*. New York: Vintage Books, 1975.

Introduction

1. Edith Lewis, *Willa Cather Living: A Personal Record* (New York: Alfred A. Knopf, 1953), 23.

2. Gaston Bachelard, *The Poetics of Space* (New York: Orion Press, 1964), xxxi.

3. Ibid., xxxiii.

4. Ibid., xiv–xv.

5. Judith Fryer, *Felicitous Space: The Imaginative Structures of Edith Wharton and Willa Cather* (Chapel Hill: University of North Carolina Press, 1986), 342.

6. Hermione Lee, *Willa Cather: Double Lives* (New York: Pantheon, 1989), 16.

7. Pablo Neruda, "We Live in a Whitmanesque Age," *New York Times* (14 April 1972): 39.

8. Gretel Ehrlich, *The Solace of Open Spaces* (New York: Penguin Books, 1985), 3.

9. Willa Cather, *My Ántonia* (Boston: Houghton Mifflin, 1954), 264. All subsequent references to this work are cited parenthetically in the text as *MA*.

10. Archives, Red Cloud, Nebraska. In June 1989, I traveled to Red Cloud and read hundreds of Cather's letters, many of which dealt with her deep feelings about the town and its inhabitants.

11. Frederick Turner, *Spirit of Place: The Making of an American Literary Landscape* (San Francisco: Sierra Club Books, 1989), ix.

12. Ibid., 145.

13. Ibid., 296.

14. Ibid., 296.

15. Italo Calvino, *The Uses of Literature* (San Diego: Harcourt Brace Jovanovich, 1982), 341.

16. Eugene Victor Walter, *Placeways: A Theory of the Human Environment* (Chapel Hill: University of North Carolina Press, 1988), 18.

17. Ibid., 13–14.

18. Ibid., 21.

19. Ibid., 21.

20. Archives, Red Cloud.

21. Louise Bogan, "American Classic," *The New Yorker* (8 August 1931): 19.

22. Willa Cather, *The Professor's House* (New York: Vintage Books, 1973), 191.

23. Yi-Fu Tuan, *Space and Place: The Perspective of Experience.* (Minneapolis: University of Minnesota Press, 1979), 203.

24. Edgar Anderson, *The Considered Landscape* (Buffalo: White Pine Press, 1985), 13.

25. L. Brent Bohlke, ed., *Willa Cather in Person: Interviews, Speeches, and Letters* (Lincoln: University of Nebraska Press, 1986), 141.

26. Ibid., 141.

27. James Woodress, *Willa Cather: A Literary Life* (Lincoln: University of Nebraska Press, 1987), 3.

28. Turner, *Spirit of Place*, 143.

29. Willa Cather, *On Writing: Critical Studies on Writing as an Art* (Lincoln: University of Nebraska Press, 1988), 109.

30. *Lucy Gayheart* represents an odd inversion of this pattern. The home Lucy longs for is in the arms of Clement, who drowns, as she drowns figu-

ratively, in the home she does not sufficiently understand. Lucy's imagined home in her lover's arms is therefore as dangerous as Emil's home in the arms of Marie Tovesky in *O Pioneers!*

31. Sharon Daloz Parks, "Home and Pilgrimmage: Companion Metaphors for Personal and Social Transformation," *Soundings* 72 (1989): 304.

32. In a Catherian twist, Claude Wheeler, in *One of Ours*, dies happy in the beloved landscape which provides his welcome exile from a repellent home.

33. Yi-Fu Tuan, *Topophilia: A Study of Environmental Perception, Attitudes, and Values* (Englewood Cliffs, N.J.: Prentice Hall, 1974), 3–33.

34. Tuan, *Space and Place: The Perspective of Experience* (Minneapolis: University of Minnesota Press, 1977), 136.

35. Vivian Gornick, "American Beauty: The Triumph of Willa Cather," *Village Voice* (10 May 1988): 33.

36. Ellen Moers, *Literary Women: The Great Writers* (Garden City, N.Y.: Doubleday & Company, 1977), 391.

37. Tuan, *Space and Place, 137.*

38. Ibid., 138.

39. Barbara Morris Caspersen, *The Flowering of Desire: Willa Cather and the Sources of Miracle.* (Ph.D. diss., Drew University, 1990). Caspersen's work represents an extended consideration of miracle and religious experience in Cather's fiction.

Chapter 1. *Alexander's Bridge*: Willa Cather's Philosophy of Composition

1. Montgomery Schyler, *Harper's Weekly* (24 May 1883): 24.

2. David Harvey, *The Condition of Post-Modernity: An Enquiry into the Origins of Cultural Change* (Oxford: Basil Blackwell, 1989), 21.

3. Cather, *On Writing*, 93.

4. David Stouck, *Willa Cather's Imagination* (Lincoln: University of Nebraska Press, 1974), 13.

5. Doris Grumbach, foreword, *O Pioneers!* by Willa Cather (Boston: Houghton Mifflin, 1988), xv.

6. Bernice Slote, introduction, *Alexander's Bridge* by Willa Cather (Lincoln: University of Nebraska Press, 1977), xxi.

7. Sharon O'Brien, introduction, *Alexander's Bridge* by Willa Cather (New York: New American Library, 1987), xix.

8. Ibid., xix–xx.

9. Ibid., xx.

10. Ibid., xxiii.

11. H. L. Mencken, "Review of *Alexander's Bridge*," *Smart Set* 38 (December 1912): 156.

12. Ibid., 156.

13. Ibid.

14. Willa Cather, *Alexander's Bridge* (Lincoln: University of Nebraska

Press, 1977), 37. All subsequent references to this work are cited parenthetically in the text as *AB*.

15. Joseph Gies, *Bridges and Men* (New York: Doubleday & Company, 1963), 226.

16. Richard J. Cook, *The Beauty of Railroad Bridges* (San Marino, Calif.: Golden West Books, 1987), 70.

17. Martin Hayden, *The Book of Bridges* (New York: Galahad Books, 1976), 100.

18. Cather, *On Writing*, 91.

19. Ibid., 92.

20. Ibid., 5.

Chapter 2. Outside the Bedroom Window:
The Laugh of the Muse in *A Lost Lady*

1. Annie Dillard, *The Writing Life* (New York: Harper & Row, 1989), 72.

2. Willa Cather, *A Lost Lady* (New York: Vintage Books, 1972), 100. All subsequent references to this work are cited parenthetically in the text as *AL*.

3. Susan Rosowski, *The Voyage Perilous: Willa Cather's Romanticism* (Lincoln: University of Nebraska Press, 1989), 117.

4. Merrill Maguire Skaggs, *After the World Broke in Two: The Later Novels of Willa Cather* (Charlottesville: University of Virginia Press), 51.

5. John T. Irwin, *Doubling and Incest: Repetition and Revenge: A Speculative Reading of Faulkner* (Baltimore: Johns Hopkins University Press, 1981), 171.

6. Woodress, *Willa Cather: A Literary Life,* 340.

7. Rosowski, *The Voyage Perilous*, 116.

8. Woodress, *Willa Cather: A Literary Life*, 341.

9. Ibid., 340.

10. Jo Ann Middleton, *Willa Cather's Modernism: A Study of Style and Technique* (Rutherford, N.J.: Fairleigh Dickinson University Press, 1990), 89.

11. Joseph Brodsky, *To Urania* (New York: Noonday Press, 1992), 70.

Chapter 3. Landscape and Possession in
The Professor's House

1. Willa Cather, *Not Under Forty* (Lincoln: University of Nebraska Press, 1988), v.

2. Cather, *On Writing*, 41–42.

3. Woodress, *Willa Cather: A Literary Life*, 223.

4. Willa Cather, *Obscure Destinies* (New York: Vintage Books, 1974), 158.

5. Woodress, *Willa Cather: A Literary Life*, 337.

6. Skaggs, *After the World Broke in Two.* In this rich and compelling work, Skaggs reads Cather's later novels as parables of how to survive in a broken world.

7. Mary Gordon, "The Silent Drama in Vuillard's Rooms," *New York Times* (13 May 1990): 1.

8. Woodress, *Willa Cather: A Literary Life*, 216.

9. Rosowski, *The Voyage Perilous*, 63.

10. Leo Marx, *The Pilot and the Passenger: Essays on Literature, Technology, and Culture in the United States* (New York: Oxford University Press, 1988), 317.

11. Willa Cather, *The Professor's House* (New York: Vintage Books, 1973), 25. All subsequent references to this work are cited parenthetically in the text as *PH*.

12. Gaston Bachelard, *The Poetics of Space* (New York: Orion Press, 1964), 239.

13. Cather, *Not Under Forty*, 77–78.

14. Woodress, *Willa Cather: A Literary Life*, 237.

15. Ibid., 297.

16. I discuss the tension between movement and stasis more fully in my chapter on *Death Comes for the Archbishop.*

17. Leon Edel, *Stuff of Sleep and Dreams: Experiments in Literary Psychology* (New York: Harper & Row, 1982), 216.

18. Cynthia K. Briggs, "Insulated Isolation: Willa Cather's Room with a View," *Cather Studies*, vol. 1, ed. by Susan J. Rosowski (Lincoln: University of Nebraska Press, 1990). Briggs's work beautifully describes Cather's need to situate her characters (and herself) in protected places that provide enlivening views.

19. Sandra M. Gilbert and Susan Gubar, *No Man's Land: The Place of the Woman Writer in the Twentieth Century,* vol. 2, *Sex Changes* (New Haven: Yale University Press, 1989), 180.

20. Willa Cather, *Death Comes for the Archbishop* (New York: Vintage Books, 1971), 3.

21. Willa Cather, *The Song of the Lark* (Boston: Houghton Mifflin, 1965), 389–90.

22. Ibid., 397.

23. Susan Rosowski, "Writing against Silences: Female Adolescent Development in the Novels of Willa Cather," *Studies in the Novel* (Spring 1989): 61.

24. Woodress, *Willa Cather: A Literary Life*, 367.

25. Rosowski, *The Voyage Perilous*, xiii.

26. Cather, *Death Comes for the Archbishop*, 18.

27. Ibid., 20.

28. Stephen Tennant, foreword, *On Writing*, by Cather, v.

29. Bachelard, *The Poetics of Space*, 184.

Chapter 4. *My Mortal Enemy*:
Willa Cather's Ballad of Exile

1. Marcus Klein, introduction, *My Mortal Enemy*, by Willa Cather, (New York: Vintage Books, 1954), v.

2. Woodress, *Willa Cather: A Literary Life*, 153

3. Cather, *Not Under Forty*, 78–79.

4. Klein, introduction, *My Mortal Enemy*, by Cather, viii.

5. Woodress, *Willa Cather: A Literary Life*, 390.

6. Willa Cather, *O Pioneers!* (Boston: Houghton Mifflin, 1941), 119.

7. Gordon Hall Gerould, *The Ballad of Tradition* (New York: Oxford Press, 1957), 86.

8. Willa Cather, *My Mortal Enemy* (New York: Vintage Books, 1954), 5. All subsequent references to this work are cited parenthetically in the text as *MME*.

9. I will discuss Latour in relation to the practice of the stations of the cross more fully in my chapter on *Death Comes for the Archbishop*.

10. Woodress, *Willa Cather: A Literary Life*, 384.

11. Francis B. Gummere, *Popular Ballad* (New York: Dover Publications, 1959), 125.

12. Evelyn Kendrick Wells, *The Ballad Tree: A Study of British and American Ballads. Their Folklore, Verse, and Music* (New York: The Ronald Press, 1950), 272.

13. Belden C. Lane, *Landscapes of the Sacred: Geography and Narrative in American Spirituality* (New York: Paulist Press, 1988), xi. Schneiders has written a foreword to Belden Lane's fascinating study of the role of landscape in American spirituality.

14. Cather, *On Writing*, 39– 40.

15. Woodress, *Willa Cather: A Literary Life*, 384 –85.

16. Willa Cather, *Obscure Destinies* (New York: Vintage Books, 1974), 158.

17. Woodress, *Willa Cather: A Literary Life*, 384.

18. Cather, *Willa Cather on Writing*, 42– 43.

19. Woodress, *Willa Cather: A Literary Life*, 384.

Chapter 5. *Death Comes for the Archbishop:*
"L'invitation du voyage!":
The Search for the Sacred Place

1. Pierre Teilhard de Chardin, *Hymn of the Universe* (New York: Harper & Row, 1965), 64.

2. Catherine Texier, "Laurie Anderson Sings the Body Electronic," *New York Times* (1 October 1989): 41.

3. W. J. Howlett, *Life of Machebeuf* (Pueblo: The Franklin Press, 1908), 116.

4. Woodress, *Willa Cather: A Literary Life*, 393.

5. Edith Lewis, *Willa Cather Living* (Athens: Ohio University Press, 1989), 139.

6. Rosowski, *The Voyage Perilous*, 161.

7. Lewis, *Willa Cather Living*, 80–81.

8. Rosowski, *The Voyage Perilous*, 164.

9. Jacques Derrida and Mustapha Tlili, eds., *For Nelson Mandela* (New York: Henry Holt, 1987), 217. Hélène Cixous's essay, "The Parting of the Cake," was written for the Derrida anthology. She discusses the influence of South African landscape on political oppression and resistance.

10. Elizabeth Hampsten, *Read This Only to Yourself: The Private Writings of Midwestern Women* (Bloomington: Indiana University Press, 1982), 36.

11. Rosowski, *The Voyage Perilous*, 165–66.

12. Ibid., 166.

13. Willa Cather, *The Kingdom of Art: Willa Cather's First Principles and Critical Statements, 1893–1896*, ed. Bernice Slote (Lincoln: University of Nebraska Press, 1966), 35.

14. Ibid.

15. Woodress, *Willa Cather: A Literary Life*, 393.

16. Howlett, *Life of Machebeuf*, 75–76.

17. Ibid., 423.

18. Ibid., 29.

19. Merrill Maguire Skaggs, "*Death Comes for the Archbishop*: Cather's Mystery and Manners," *American Literature* 57 (October 1985): 404.

20. Clinton Keeler, "Narrative without Accent: Willa Cather and Puvis de Chavannes," *American Quarterly* 17 (Spring 1965): 124.

21. E. A. Carmean, *Helen Frankenthuler: A Paintings Retrospective* (New York: Harry N. Abrams, 1989), 70.

22. Ibid.

23. Ibid., 72.

24. Ibid.

25. Howlett, *Life of Machebeuf*, 22.

26. Ibid., 25.

27. Ibid., 33.

28. Elizabeth Shepley Sergeant, *Willa Cather: A Memoir* (Philadelphia: J. B. Lippincott, 1953), 236.

29. Willa Cather, *Death Comes for the Archbishop* (New York: Vintage, 1971), 274. All subsequent references to this work are cited parenthetically in the text as *DC*.

30. Rosowski, *The Voyage Perilous*, 172.

31. Ibid., 167.

32. Ibid.

33. Henri J. Nouwen, *The Genesee Diary: Report from a Trappist Monastery* (Garden City, N.Y.: Doubleday & Company, 1976), 36.

34. Pierre Teilhard de Chardin, *Hymn to the Universe*, 64.

35. Lane, *Landscapes of the Sacred*, 37.

36. Mircea Eliade, *The Sacred and the Profane: The Nature of Religion* (New York: Harper & Row, 1959), 37.

37. Ibid.

38. Mircea Eliade, *The Myth of the Eternal Return or, Cosmos and History* (Princeton: Princeton University Press, 1954), 12.

39. Mircea Eliade, *The Sacred and the Profane*, 41.

40. Ibid.

41. Wallace Stevens, *The Palm at the End of the Mind* (New York: Vintage Books, 1967), 371.

42. Holly Stevens, ed., *Letters of Wallace Stevens* (New York: Alfred A. Knopf, 1966), 381.

Chapter 6. *Shadows on the Rock*: The Imagination in Exile

1. Susan Rosowski, "Willa Cather's Female Landscapes: *The Song of the Lark* and *Lucy Gayheart*," *Women's Studies* 11 (December 1984): 238.

2. Willa Cather, *Shadows on the Rock* (New York: Vintage Books, 1971), 25. All subsequent references to this work are cited parenthetically in the text as *SR*.

3. Willa Cather, *Death Comes for the Archbishop*, 39.

4. Edith Lewis, *Willa Cather Living* (Athens: Ohio University Press, 1989), 160.

5. Nouwen, *The Genesee Diary*, 73.

6. Parks, "Home and Pilgrimage," 301.

7. Ibid., 300.

8. Ibid.

9. Susan A. Hallgarth, "Archetypal Patterns in *Shadows on the Rock*," *Colby Library Quarterly* 24, no. 3 (September 1988): 134.

10. Howlett, *Life of Machebeuf*, 35.

11. Woodress, *Willa Cather: A Literary Life*, 425.

12. Lewis, *Willa Cather Living*, 158.

13. Parks, "Home and Pilgrimage," 301–2.

14. Woodress, *Willa Cather: A Literary Life*, 412.

15. Ibid., 413.

16. Ibid.

17. Lewis, *Willa Cather Living*, 152.

18. Woodress, *Willa Cather: A Literary Life*, 423.

19. Lewis, *Willa Cather Living*, 155.

20. Ibid., 163.

21. Woodress, *Willa Cather: A Literary Life*, 422.

22. Lewis, *Willa Cather Living*, 155.

23. Woodress, *Willa Cather. A Literary Life*, 434.

24. Ibid., 429.

Conclusion

1. Willa Cather, *Sapphira and the Slave Girl* (New York: Vintage Books, 1975), 273–74. All subsequent references to this work are cited parenthetically in the text as *SSG*.

2. Toni Morrison, *Playing in the Dark: Whiteness and the Literary Imagination* (Cambridge, Mass.: Harvard University Press, 1992), 23.

3. Bernice Slote, ed., *The Kingdom of Art: Willa Cather's First Principles and Critical Statements, 1893–1896* (Lincoln: University of Nebraska Press, 1966), 445.

Bibliography

Works by Willa Cather

Cather, Willa. *24 Stories*. Edited by Sharon O'Brien. New York: New American Library, 1987.

———. *Alexander's Bridge*. Lincoln: University of Nebraska Press, 1977.

———. *A Lost Lady*. New York: Vintage Books, 1972.

———. *April Twilights*. Edited by Bernice Slote. Lincoln: University of Nebraska Press, 1962.

———. *Collected Short Fiction: 1892–1912*. Edited by Virginia Faulkner. Lincoln: University of Nebraska Press, 1965.

———. *Death Comes for the Archbishop*. New York: Vintage Books, 1971.

———. *Five Stories*. New York: Vintage Books, 1956.

———. *Great Short Works of Willa Cather*. Edited by Robert K. Miller. New York: Harper & Row, 1989.

———. *The Kingdom of Art: Willa Cather's First Principles and Critical Statements, 1893–1896*. Edited by Bernice Slote. Lincoln: University of Nebraska Press, 1966.

———. *Lucy Gayheart*. New York: Alfred A. Knopf, 1935.

———. *My Ántonia*. Boston: Houghton Mifflin, 1954.

———. *My Mortal Enemy*. New York: Vintage Books, 1954.

———. *Not Under Forty*. Lincoln: University of Nebraska Press, 1988.

———. *Obscure Destinies*. New York: Vintage Books, 1974.

———. *The Old Beauty and Others*. New York: Vintage Books, 1976.

———. *On Writing: Critical Studies on Writing as an Art*. Lincoln: University of Nebraska Press, 1988. Forward by Stephen Tennant, 1944.

———. *One of Ours*. New York: Vintage Books, 1950.

------. *O Pioneers!* Boston: Houghton Mifflin, 1941.

------. *The Professor's House.* New York: Vintage Books, 1973.

------. *Sapphira and the Slave Girl.* New York: Vintage Books, 1975.

------. *Shadows on the Rock.* New York: Vintage Books, 1971.

------. *The Song of the Lark.* Boston: Houghton Mifflin, 1965.

------. *The Troll Garden.* New York: New American Library, 1984.

------. *Uncle Valentine and Other Stories: Willa Cather's Uncollected Short Fiction, 1915–1924.* Edited by Bernice Slote. Lincoln: University of Nebraska Press, 1986.

------. *Willa Cather in Europe: Her Own Story of the First Journey.* Edited by George N. Kates. Lincoln: University of Nebraska Press, 1988.

------. *The World and the Parish: Willa Cather's Articles and Reviews, 1893–1902.* Edited by William M. Curtin. Lincoln: University of Nebraska Press, 1970.

------. *Youth and the Bright Medusa.* New York: Vintage Books, 1975.

Works on Cather and Literary Theory

Abel, Elizabeth. *The Voyage In: Fiction of Female Development.* Hanover, N.H.: University of New England, 1983.

Allen, Walter. *The Urgent West.* New York: E. P. Dutton, 1969.

Ammons, Elizabeth. *Conflicting Stories: American Writers at the Turn into the Twentieth Century.* New York: Oxford University Press, 1991.

Arnold, Marilyn. *Willa Cather's Short Fiction.* Athens: Ohio University Press, 1984.

------, ed. *Willa Cather: A Reference Guide.* Boston: G. K. Hall, 1986.

Auchincloss, Louis. *Pioneers and Caretakers: A Study of Nine American Women Writers.* Minneapolis: University Press, 1958.

Barfield, Owen. *Poetic Diction.* Middletown, Conn.: Wesleyan University Press, 1973.

Beebe, Maurice. *Ivory Tower, and Sacred Founts: The Artist as Hero in Fiction from Goethe to Joyce.* New York: New York University Press, 1964.

Beeck, Frans Josef van. *God Encountered: A Contemporary Catholic Systematic Theology.* San Francisco: Harper & Row, 1989.

Bercovitch, Sacvan, and Myra Jehlen, eds. *Ideology and Classic American Literature.* Cambridge: Cambridge University Press, 1986.

Bennett, Mildred R. *The World of Willa Cather.* Lincoln: University of Nebraska Press, 1961.

Berrigan, Daniel, and Margaret Parker. *Stations: The Way of the Cross.* San Francisco: Harper & Row, 1989.

Bloom, Edward A., and Lillian D. Bloom. *Willa Cather's Gift of Sympathy.* Carbondale: Southern Illinois University Press, 1962.

Bloom, Harold. *Modern Critical Views: Willa Cather.* New York: Chelsea House, 1985.

Bohlke, L. Brent, ed. *Willa Cather in Person: Interviews, Speeches, and Letters.* Lincoln: University of Nebraska Press, 1986.

Brodsky, Joseph. *To Urania.* New York: Noonday Press, 1992.

Brooks, Van Wyck. *The Writer in America.* New York: E. P. Dutton, 1953.

Brown, E. K. *Rhythm in the Novel.* Toronto: University of Toronto Press, 1950.

———. *Willa Cather: A Critical Biography.* Completed by Leon Edel. New York: Avon Books, 1980.

Brown, Marion Marsh, and Ruth Crone. *Only One Point of the Compass: Willa Cather in the Northeast.* Danbury, Conn.: Archer Editions Press, 1980.

Bruccoli, Matthew J., and Margaret M. Duggan, eds. *Correspondence of F. Scott Fitzgerald.* New York: Random House, 1980.

Byrne, Kathleen D., and Richard C. Snyder. *Chrysalis: Willa Cather in Pittsburgh, 1896–1906.* Pittsburgh: Historical Society of Western Pennsylvania, 1980.

Callander, Marilyn Berg. *Willa Cather and the Fairy Tale.* Ann Arbor, Mich.: UMI Research Press, 1989.

Calvino, Italo. *The Uses of Literature.* Translated by Patrick Creagh. San Diego: Harcourt Brace Jovanovich, 1982.

Carmean, E. A., Jr. *Helen Frankenthuler: A Paintings Retrospective.* New York: Harry N. Abrams, 1989.

Child, Francis James. *English and Scottish Popular Ballads.* Boston: Houghton Mifflin, 1932.

Coetzee, J. M. *White Writing: On the Culture of Letters in South Africa.* New Haven: Yale University Press, 1988.

Cooperman, Stanley. *World War I and the American Novel.* Baltimore: Johns Hopkins University Press, 1967.

Cowley, Malcolm, Edited by *After the Genteel Tradition.* Gloucester, Mass.: Peter Smith, 1959.

Curtin, William, ed. *The World and the Parish.* Lincoln: University of Nebraska Press, 1970.

Daiches, David. *Willa Cather: A Critical Introduction.* Ithaca: Cornell University Press, 1951.

Derrida, Jacques, and Mustapha Tlili, eds. *For Nelson Mandela.* New York: Henry Holt, 1987.

Detweiler, Robert. *Breaking the Fall: Religious Readings of Contemporary Fiction.* San Francisco: Harper & Row, 1989.

Dillard, Annie. *The Writing Life.* New York: Harper & Row, 1989.

Donovan, Josephine. *After the Fall: The Demeter-Persephone Myth in Wharton, Cather, and Glasgow*. University Park: The Pennsylavania State University Press, 1989.

Duncan, Robert. *The Opening of the Field*. New York: New Directions, 1960.

Edel, Leon. *Stuff of Sleep and Dreams: Experiments in Literary Psychology*. New York: Harper & Row, 1982.

Eliade, Mircea. *The Myth of the Eternal Return or, Cosmos and History*. Princeton: Princeton University Press, 1954.

————. *The Sacred and the Profane: The Nature of Religion*. New York: Harper & Row, 1959.

Ellmann, Richard, and Robert O'Clair, eds. *The Norton Anthology of Modern Poetry*. 2d ed. New York: W. W. Norton, 1988.

Faderman, Lillian. *Surpassing the Love of Men*. New York: William Morrow, 1981.

Fiorenza, Elizabeth Schussler. *In Memory of Her: A Feminist Theological Reconstruction of Christian Origins*. New York: Crossroad, 1987.

Fisher, Philip. *Hard Facts: Setting and Form in the American Novel*. Oxford: Oxford University Press, 1985.

French, Warren, Edited by *The Twenties: Fiction, Poetry, Drama*. Deland, Fla.: Everett Edwards, 1975.

Frye, Northrup. *Anatomy of Criticism: Four Essays*. Princeton: Princeton University Press, 1957.

Gennep, Arnold van. *The Rites of Passage*. Chicago: University of Chicago Press, 1960.

Gerber, Philip. *Willa Cather*. Boston: Twayne Publishers, 1975.

Gerould, Gordon Hall. *The Ballad Tradition*. New York: Oxford University Press, 1957.

Gianonne, Richard. *Music in Willa Cather's Fiction*. Lincoln: University of Nebraska Press, 1968.

Gilbert, Sandra M., and Susan Gubar. *No Man's Land: The Place of the Woman Writer in the Twentieth Century*. Vol. 2, *Sex Changes*. New Haven: Yale University Press, 1989.

Grumbach, Doris. Foreword. *O Pioneers!*, by Willa Cather. Boston: Houghton Mifflin, 1988.

Gummere, Francis B. *Popular Ballad*. New York: Dover Publications, 1959.

Hampsten, Elizabeth. *Read This Only to Yourself: The Private Writings of Midwestern Women*. Bloomington: Indiana University Press, 1982.

Harvey, David. *The Condition of Postmodernity: An Enquiry into the Origins of Cultural Change*. Oxford: Basil Blackwell, 1989.

Hatcher, Harlan. *Creating the Modern American Novel*. New York: Russell & Russell, 1965.

Heilbrun, Carolyn G. *Writing a Woman's Life*. New York: W. W. Norton, 1988.

Hernardi, Paul. *Beyond Genre: New Directions in Literary Classification.* Ithaca: Cornell University Press, 1972.

Horgan, Paul. *The Centuries of Santa Fe.* Santa Fe, N.M.: William Gannon, 1976.

———. *Lamy of Santa Fe.* New York: Farrar, Straus, and Giroux, 1975.

Howlett, W. J. *Life of Machebeuf.* Pueblo, Colo.: The Franklin Press, 1908.

Huf, Linda. *A Portrait of the Artist as a Young Woman: The Writer as Heroine in American Literature.* New York: Frederick Unger, 1983.

Irwin, John T. *Doubling and Incest: Repition and Revenge: A Speculative Reading of Faulkner.* Baltimore: Johns Hopkins University Press, 1981.

Jacobus, Mary, ed. *Women Writing and Writing about Women.* New York: Barnes & Noble, 1979.

Kazin, Alfred. *On Native Grounds.* New York: Reynal & Hitchcock, 1942.

Kirschke, James J. *Willa Cather and Six Writers from the Great War.* New York: University Press of America, 1991.

Lawrence, D. H. *Studies in Classic American Literature.* Garden City, N.Y.: Doubleday & Company, 1923.

Lee, Hermoine. *Willa Cather: Double Lines.* New York: Pantheon Books, 1989.

Lewis, Edith. *Willa Cather Living.* Athens: Ohio University Press, 1989.

Lubbock, Percy. *The Craft of Fiction.* New York: Peter Smith, 1921.

Macauley, Robie, and George Lanning. *Technique in Fiction.* New York: Harper & Row, 1964.

Mainiero, Lina, ed. *American Women Writers.* New York: Frederick Unger, 1979.

Marcus, Jane. *Art and Anger: Reading Like a Woman.* Columbus: Ohio State University Press, 1988.

Marx, Leo. *The Machine in the Garden: Technology and the Pastoral Ideal in America.* Oxford: Oxford University Press, 1964.

———. *The Pilot and the Passenger: Essays on Literature, Technology, and Culture in the United States.* New York: Oxford University Press, 1988.

Matthiessen, F. O. *America Renaissance: Art and Expression in the Age of Emerson and Whitman.* Oxford: Oxford University Press, 1968.

McClure, S. S. *My Autobiography.* New York: Frederick A. Stokes Company, 1914.

Middleton, Jo Ann. *Willa Cather's Modernism: A Study of Style and Technique.* Rutherford, N.J.: Fairleigh Dickinson University Press, 1990.

Miller, James E., Jr. *Miracles of Perception: The Art of Willa Cather.* Charlottesville: Alderman Library, University of Virginia, 1980.

Moers, Ellen. *Literary Women: The Great Writers.* Garden City, N.Y.: Doubleday & Company, 1977.

Morrison, Toni. *Playing in the Dark: Whiteness and the Literary Imagination.* Cambridge: Harvard University Press, 1992.

Murphy, John J. *Critical Essays on Willa Cather*. Boston: G. K. Hall, 1984.

———, ed. *Five Essays on Willa Cather*. North Andover, Mass.: Merrimack College, 1974.

———, ed. *Literature and Belief: Willa Cather Issue*. Provo, Utah: Brigham Young University Press, 1988.

———. *My Ántonia: The Road Home*. Boston: Twayne Publishers, 1989.

Nelson, Robert J. *Willa Cather and France: In Search of the Lost Language*. Urbana: University of Illinois Press, 1988.

Newman, Charles. *The Post-Modern Aura: The Act of Fiction in an Age of Inflation*. Evanston, Ill.: Northwestern University Press, 1985.

Nouwen, Henri J. *The Genesee Diary: Report from a Trappist Monastery*. Garden City, N.Y.: Doubleday & Company, 1976.

O'Brien, Sharon. *Willa Cather: The Emerging Voice*. New York: Oxford University Press, 1987.

———. Introduction. *Alexander's Bridge*, by Willa Cather. New York: New American Library, 1988.

Olsen, Tillie. *Silences*. New York: Delacourt Press/Seymour Lawrence, 1978.

Ostier, Marianne. *Jewels and the Woman*. New York: Horizon Press, 1958.

Oswalt, Conrad E. *After Eden: The Secularization of American Space in the Fiction of Willa Cather and Theodore Dreiser*. Lewisburg, Pa.: Bucknell University Press, 1990.

Power, David N. *Unsearchable Riches: The Symbolic Nature of Liturgy*. New York: Pueblo Publishing, 1984.

Pers, Mona. *Willa Cather's Children*. Stockholm, Sweden: Almquist & Wilhsell, 1975.

Person, Leland S., Jr. *Aesthetic Headaches: Women and Masculine Poetics in Poe, Melville, and Hawthorne*. Athens: University of Georgia Press, 1988.

Pollock, Griselda. *Vision of Difference: Femininity, Feminism, and the Histories of Art*. London: Routledge, 1988.

Porter, Katherine Anne. *The Days Before*. New York: Harcourt, Brace and Company, 1952.

Quinn, Arthur Hobson. *The Literature of the American People*. New York: Appleton-Century-Crofts, 1951.

Quaife, Milo Milton, Edited by *Kit Carson's Autobiography*. Lincoln: University of Nebraska Press, 1966.

Randall, John H. *The Landscape and the Looking Glass: Willa Cather's Search for Value*. Boston: Houghton Mifflin, 1960.

Rank, Otto. *The Double: A Psychoanalytic Study*. Translated by Harry Tucker, Jr., New York: New American Library, 1971.

Ransom, John Crowe. *The New Criticism*. Norfolk, Conn.: New Directions, 1941.

Rapin, Rene. *Willa Cather.* New York: R. M. McBride, 1930.

Rich, Adrienne. *A Wild Patience Has Taken Me This Far.* New York: W. W. Norton, 1981.

Robinson, Phyllis. *Willa: The Life of Willa Cather.* Garden City, N.Y.: Doubleday and Company, 1983.

Romines, Ann. *The Home Plot: Women Writing & Domestic Ritual.* Amherst: University of Massachusetts Press, 1992.

Rosowski, Susan J., ed. *Approaches to Teaching Cather's My Ántonia.* New York: Modern Language Association of America, 1989.

————. *The Voyage Perilous: Willa Cather's Romanticism.* Lincoln: University of Nebraska Press, 1986.

Ross, Nancy Wilson. *Westward the Women.* San Francisco: North Point Press, 1985.

Ryder, Mary Ruth. *Willa Cather and Myth: The Search for a New Parnassus.* Lewiston: The Edwin Mellen Press, 1990.

Sacken, Jeanee P. *"A Certain Slant of Light": Aesthetics of First Person Narration in Gide and Cather.* New York: Garland, 1985.

Schroeter, James, ed. *Willa Cather and Her Critics.* Ithaca: Cornell University Press, 1967.

Sergeant, Elizabeth Shepley. *Willa Cather: A Memoir.* Philadelphia: J. B. Lippincott, 1953.

Sherman, Stuart. *Critical Woodcuts.* New York: Charles Scribner's Sons, 1926.

Shinley-Smith, H. *The World's Great Bridges.* New York: Harper & Row, 1953, 1964.

Slote, Bernice, and Virginia Faulkner, eds. *The Art of Willa Cather.* Lincoln: University of Nebraska Press, 1974.

Skaggs, Merrill Maguire. *After the World Broke in Two: The Later Novels of Willa Cather.* Charlottesville: University Press of Virginia, 1990.

Stevens, Holly, ed. *Letters of Wallace Stevens.* New York: Alfred A. Knopf, 1966.

Stouck, David. *Willa Cather's Imagination.* Lincoln: University of Nebraska Press, 1975.

Tanner, Tony. *Scenes of Nature, Signs of Men.* Cambridge: Cambridge University Press, 1987.

Teilhard de Chardin, Pierre. *Hymn of the Universe.* New York: Harper & Row, 1965.

Thomas, Susie. *Willa Cather.* Savage, Md.: Barnes & Noble, 1990.

Todd, Janet, ed. *Gender and Literary Voice.* New York: Holmes and Meier, 1980.

Turner, Victor. *Dramas, Fields, and Metaphors: Symbolic Action in Human Society.* Ithaca: Cornell University Press, 1974.

Veeder, William, and Susan M. Griffin, eds. *The Art of Criticism: Henry James on the Theory and Practice of Fiction.* Chicago: University of Chicago Press, 1986.

118   BIBLIOGRAPHY

Wells, Evelyn Kendrick. *The Ballad Tree: A Study of British and American Ballads, Their Folklore, Verse, and Music.* New York: The Ronald Press, 1950.

Welty, Eudora. *The Eye of the Story.* New York: Random House, 1977.

Woods, Lucia. *Willa Cather: A Pictorial Memoir.* Photos. Text by Bernice Slote. Lincoln: University of Nebraska Press, 1973.

Woodress, James. *Willa Cather: A Literary Life.* Lincoln: University of Nebraska Press, 1987.

———. *Willa Cather: Her Life and Art.* New York: Pegasus, 1970.

Zinsser, William, ed. *Inventing the Truth: The Art and Craft of Memoir.* Boston: Houghton Mifflin, 1987.

Works on Space, Place, and Architecture

Anderson, Edgar. *The Considered Landscape.* Buffalo, N.Y.: White Pine Press, 1985.

Bachelard, Gaston. *The Poetics of Space.* New York: Orion Press, 1964.

Cook, Richard J. *The Beauty of Railroad Bridges.* San Marino, Calif.: Golden West Books, 1987.

Doig, Ivan. *This House of Sky: Landscape of a Western Mind.* New York: Harcourt Brace Jovanovich, 1978.

Ehrlich, Gretel. *The Solace of Open Spaces.* New York: Penguin Books, 1985.

Frazier, Ian. *The Great Plains.* New York: Farrar, Straus, and Giroux, 1989.

Fryer, Judith. *Felicitous Space: The Imaginative Structures of Edith Wharton and Willa Cather.* Chapel Hill: University of North Carolina Press, 1986.

Gies, Joseph. *Bridges and Men.* New York: Doubleday & Company, 1963.

Gordon, J. E. *Structures: Or Why Things Don't Fall Down.* Reading, England: University of Reading Press, 1978.

Grumbach, Doris. Introduction. *O Pioneers!* by Willa Cather. Boston: Houghton Mifflin, 1988.

Hayden, Martin. *The Book of Bridges.* New York: Galahad Books, 1976.

Horgan, Paul. *A Writer's Eye: Field Notes and Watercolors.* New York: Harry N. Abrams, 1988.

Huxtable, Ada Louise. *Architecture, Anyone?* Berkeley: University of California Press, 1986.

Kazin, Alfred. *A Writer's America: Landscapes in Literature.* New York: Alfred A. Knopf, 1988.

Kolodny, Annette. *The Land Before Her: Fantasy and Experience of the American Frontiers, 1630–1860.* Chapel Hill: University of North Carolina Press, 1984.

Lane, Belden C. *Landscapes of the Sacred: Geography and Narrative in American Spirituality*. New York: Paulist Press, 1988.

Lehrman, Fredric. *The Sacred Landscape*. Berkeley, Calif.: Celestial Arts, 1988.

McGregor, Gaile. *The Noble Savage in the New World Garden: Notes Toward a Syntatics of Place*. Toronto: University of Toronto Press, 1988.

Mulvey, Laura. *Visual and Other Pleasures*. Bloomington: Indiana University Press, 1989.

Nelson, Cary. *The Incarnate Word: Literature as Verbal Space*. Urbana: University of Illinois Press, 1973.

Norberg-Schulz, Christian. *Architecture: Meaning and Place*. New York: Electa/Rizzoli, 1988.

Norwood, Vera, and Janice Mark, eds. *The Desert Is No Lady: Southwestern Landscapes in Women's Writing and Art*. New Haven: Yale University Press, 1987.

Petroski, Henry. *To Engineer Is Human: The Role of Failure in Successful Design*. New York: St. Martin's Press, 1985.

Plowden, David. *Bridges: The Spans of North American*. New York: W. W. Norton, 1974.

Sears, John F. *Sacred Places: American Tourist Attractions in the Nineteenth Century*. New York: Oxford University Press, 1989.

Sizemore, Christine Wick. *A Female Vision of the City: London in the Novels of Five British Women*. Knoxville: University of Tennessee Press, 1989.

Stoddart, D. R. *On Geography*. London: Basil Blackwell, 1986.

Tuan, Yi-Fu. *Landscapes of Fear*. Minneapolis: University of Minnesota Press, 1979.

———. *Space and Place: The Perspective of Experience*. Minneapolis: University of Minnesota Press, 1977.

Turner, Frederick. *Spirit of Place: The Making of an American Literary Landscape*. San Francisco: Sierra Club Books, 1989.

Walter, Eugene Victor. *Placeways: A Theory of the Human Environment*. Chapel Hill: University of North Carolina Press, 1988.

Articles

Adams, Theodore S. "Willa Cather's *My Mortal Enemy*: The Concise Presentation of Scene, Character, and Theme." *Colby Literary Quarterly* 10 (September 1973): 138–48.

Anderson, Quentin. "Willa Cather: Her Masquerade." *New Republic* 154 (27 November 1965): 29–31.

Arnold, M. "Coming Willa Cather!" *Women's Studies* 11 (December 1984): 247–60.

Bash, James R. "Willa Cather and the Anathema of Materialism." *Colby Library Quarterly* 10 (September 1973): 157–68.

Benet, Laura. "Review of *The Professor's House*." Commonweal 3 (2 December 1925): 108–9.

Bloom, Edward. "Father Mansfield." In *Five Essays on Willa Cather*, edited by John J. Murphy. North Andover, Mass.: Merrimack College, 1974.

Bogan, Louise. "American Classic." *The New Yorker* (8 August 1931) 19–22.

Booth, Wayne C. "Distance and Point of View." In *The Theory of the Novel*, edited by Philip Stevick. New York: Free Press, 1967.

Brennen, Joseph X. "Willa Cather and Her Music." *University Review* 31 (Spring 1965): 175–83.

———. "Music and Willa Cather." *University Review* 31 (Summer 1965): 257–64.

Briggs, Cynthia K. "Insulated Isolation: Willa Cather's Room with a View." In *Cather Studies*, vol. 1, edited by Susan J. Rosowski. Lincoln: University of Nebraska Press, 1990.

Brown, E. K. "Homage to Willa Cather." *Yale Review* 36 (Autumn 1946): 77–92.

———. "Willa Cather." In *Willa Cather and Her Critics*, edited by James Schroeter. Ithaca: Cornell University Press, 1967.

Carroll, Lathrobe. "Willa Sibert Cather." *Bookman* 53 (May 1921): 212–13.

Cather, Willa. "Nebraska: The End of the First Cycle." *Nation* 116 (5 September 1923): 236–38.

Comeau, Paul. "Willa Cather's Lucy Gayheart: A Long Perspective." *Prairie Schooner* 55 (Spring–Summer 1981): 199–209.

Cousineau, Diane. "Division and Difference in *A Lost Lady*." *Women's Studies* 11 (December 1984): 305–22.

Curtin, William. "Willa Cather: Individualism and Style." *Colby Library Quarterly* 8 (June 1968): 36–58.

Doughty, Howard N., Jr. "Miss Cather as Critic." *Nation* 169 (24 September 1947): 304.

Eichorn, Harry B. "A Falling Out with Love: *My Mortal Enemy*." *Colby Library Quarterly* 10 (September 1973): 121–38.

Feld, Rose C. "Restlessness Such as Ours Does Not Make for Beauty." Interview with Willa Cather. *New York Times* (21 December 1924): 23.

Flax, Jane. "Postmodernism and Gender Relations in Feminist Theory." *Signs* 12, no. 4 (Summer 1987): 621–44.

Friedman, Norman. "Point of View in Fiction: The Development of a Critical Concept." In *The Theory of the Novel*, edited by Philip Stevick. New York: Free Press, 1967.

Gelfant, Blanche H. "The Forgotten Reaping-Hook: Sex in *My Ántonia*." *American Literature* 43 (March 1971): 60–82.

Geismar, Maxwell. "Willa Cather in the Wilderness." In *Willa Cather and Her Critics*, edited by James Schroeter. Ithaca: Cornell University Press, 1967.

Gerber, Philip. "Willa Cather and the Big Red Rock." *College English* 19 (January 1958): 152–57.

Gish, Robert F. "Paul Hogan and the Biography of Place." *Prairie Schooner* 55 (Spring–Summer 1981): 226–32.

Gordon, Mary. "The Silent Drama in Vuillard's Rooms." *New York Times* (13 May 1990): sec 2:1.

Gornick, Vivian. "American Beauty: The Triumph of Willa Cather." *Village Voice* (10 May 1988): 31–35.

Greene, George William. "Willa Cather at Mid-Century." *Thought* 32 (Winter 1958): 577–92.

Griffiths, Frederick T. "The Woman Warrior: Willa Cather and *One of Ours*." *Women's Studies* 11 (December 1984): 261–85.

Grumbach, Doris. "A Study of the Small Room in *The Professor's House*." *Women's Studies* 11 (December 1984): 327–45.

Hallgarth, Susan A. "Archetypal Patterns in *Shadows on the Rock*." *Colby Library Quarterly* 24, no. 3 (September 1988): 133–41.

Hamner, Eugenie Lambert. "The Unknown Well-Known Child in Cather's Last Novel." *Women's Studies* 11 (December 1984): 347–57.

Hampton, Benjamin B. "The Author and the Motion Picture." *Bookman* 53 (May 1921): 216–25.

Hicks, Granville. "The Case against Willa Cather." In *Willa Cather and Her Critics*, edited by James Schroeter. Ithaca: Cornell University Press, 1967.

James, Henry. "The House of Fiction." In *The Theory of the Novel*, edited by Philip Stevick. New York: Free Press, 1967.

Jones, Howard Mumford. "The Novels of Willa Cather." *Saturday Review* 18 (6 August 1938): 3–4, 16.

Kahler, Erich. "The Transformation of Modern Fiction." *Comparative Fiction* 7, no. 2 (1955): 121–28.

Keeler, Clinton. "Narrative without Accent: Willa Cather and Puvis de Chavannes." *American Quarterly* 17 (Spring 1965): 119–26.

Kronenberger, Louis. "Willa Cather." *Bookman* 74 (October 1931): 134–40.

Lutwack, Leonard. "Mixed and Uniform Prose Styles in the Novel." In *The Theory of the Novel*, edited by Philip Stevick. New York: Free Press, 1967.

Maxfield, J. F. "Strategies of Self-Deception in Willa Cather's *The Professor's House*." *Studies in the Novel* 16 (Spring 1984): 72–84.

Mencken, H. L. "Review of *Alexander's Bridge*." *Smart Set* 38 (December 1912): 156–57.

Moorhead, Elizabeth. "The Novelist." In *Willa Cather and Her Critics*, edited by James Schroeter. Ithaca: Cornell University Press, 1967.

Morrow, Nancy. "Willa Cather's *A Lost Lady* and the Nineteenth-Century Novel of Adultery." *Women's Studies* 11 (December 1984): 287–303.

Murphy, John J. "Cooper, Cather, and the Downward Path to Progress." *Prairie Schooner* 55 (Spring–Summer 1981): 168–84.

———. "The Respectable Romantic and the Unwed Mother: Class Consciousness in *My Ántonia*." *Colby Library Quarterly* 10 (September 1973): 149–56.

Neruda, Pablo. "We Live in a Whitmanesque Age." *New York Times* (14 April 1972): 39.

O'Brien, Sharon. "Mother, Daughter, and the 'Art Necessity': Willa Cather and the Creative Process." In *American Novelists—Revisited: Essays in Feminist Criticism*, edited by Fritz Fleishman. Boston: Hall, 1982.

Pannill, Linda. "Willa Cather's Artist-Heroines." *Women's Studies* 11 (December 1984): 223–32.

Parks, Sharon Daloz. "Home and Pilgrimage: Companion Metaphors for Personal and Social Transformation." *Soundings* 72 (Summer–Fall 1989): 299–315.

Pearson, Norman Holmes. "Willa Cather on Writing." *Saturday Review* 32 (8 October 1949): 37.

Poore, Charles. "The Last Stories of Willa Cather." *New York Times Book Review* (12 September 1948): 3.

Porter, Katherine Anne. "An Calm Pure Art of Willa Cather." *New York Times Book Review* (25 September 1949): 1.

Price, Reynolds. "Men Creating Women." *New York Times Book Review* (9 November 1986): 1, 16,18, 20.

Rosowski, S. J. "Narrative Technique in Cather's *My Mortal Enemy*." *Journal of Narrative Technique* 8 (1978): 141–49.

———. "Willa Cather—A Pioneer in Art: *O Pioneers!* and *My Ántonia*." *Prairie Schooner* 55 (Spring–Summer 1981): 141–55.

———. "Willa Cather's Female Landscapes: *The Song of the Lark* and *Lucy Gayheart*." *Women's Studies* 11 (December 1984): 233–46.

———. "Writing against Silences: Female Adolescent Development in the Novels of Willa Cather." *Studies in the Novel* 32 (Spring 1989): 60–77.

Salo, Alice Bell. "*The Professor's House* and *Le Mannequinn d'Osier*: A Note on Willa Cather's Narrative Technique." *Studies in American Fiction* 8 (1978): 229–31.

Schroeter, James. "Willa Cather and *The Professor's House*." *Yale Review* 54 (June 1965): 494–512.

Schwind, Jean. "The Benda Illustrations to *My Ántonia*: Cather's Silent Supplement to Jim Burden's Narrative." *PMLA* 100, no. 1 (January 1985): 51–67.

Shroder, Maurice Z. "The Nouveau Romance and the Tradition of the Novel." *Romantic Review* 17, no. 3 (October 1966): 200–14.

Skaggs, Merrill Maguire. "A Glance into *The Professor's House*: Inward and Outward Bound." *Renascence* 39 (Spring 1987): 422–28.

———. "*Death Comes for the Archbishop*: Cather's Mystery and Manners." *American Literature* 57 (October 1985): 395– 406.

———. "Poe's Shadow on *Alexander's Bridge*." *Mississippi Quarterly* 35 (Fall 1982): 365–74.

———. "Willa Cather's Experimental Southern Novel." *Mississippi Quarterly* 35, no. 4 (Winter 1981): 3–14.

Slote, Bernice. Introduction. *Alexander's Bridge,* by Willa Cather. Lincoln: University of Nebraska Press, 1977.

———. "Willa Cather." In *Sixteen Modern American Writers,* edited by Jackson R. Bryer. Durham, N.C.: Duke University Press, 1974.

———. "Willa Cather." In *Willa Cather and Her Critics,* edited by James Schroeter. Ithaca: Cornell University Press, 1967.

Texier, Catherine. "Laurie Anderson Sings the Body Electronic." *New York Times* (1 October 1989): sec. 2:1, 41.

West, Rebecca. "The Classic Artist." In *Willa Cather and Her Critics,* edited by James Schroeter. Ithaca: Cornell University Press, 1967.

Wild, Barbara. " 'The Thing Not Named' in *The Professor's House*." *Western American Literature* 12 (1978): 263–74.

Wilson, Edmund. "Two Novels of Willa Cather." In *Willa Cather and Her Critics,* edited by James Schroeter. Ithaca: Cornell University Press, 1967.

Winsten, Archer. "A Defense of Willa Cather." *Bookman* 74 (March 1932): 634 – 41.

Zabel, Morton Davwen. "Willa Cather." *Nation* 164 (14 June 1947): 713–16.

Dissertations

Bell, Alice. "Through the Professor's Window: Reading Willa Cather's Novel Demeuble." Ph.D. diss., University of Minnesota, 1986.

Bohlke, Landall Brent. " 'Seeking is Finding': Willa Cather and Religion." Ph.D. diss., University of Nebraska, Lincoln, 1982.

Callander, Marilyn Berg. "Willa Cather's Use of Fairy Tales." Ph.D. diss., Drew University, 1987.

Cassai, Mary Ann. "Symbolic Techniques in Selected Novels of Willa Cather." Ph.D. diss., New York University, 1978.

Doughaday, Charles H. "Willa Cather's 'Happy Experimenting': Artistic Fusion of Theme and Structure." Ph.D. diss., University of Kentucky, 1967.

Lambert, Maude Eugenie. "Theme and Craftsmanship in Willa Cather's Novels." Ph.D. diss., University of North Carolina, 1965.

MacDonald, Phyllis Black. "The Composed Image: The House and the Garden in the Fiction of Willa Cather." Ph.D. diss., West Virginia University, 1985.

Massey, David G. "Simplicity with Suggestiveness in Willa Cather's Revised and Republished Fiction." Ph.D. diss., Drew University, 1979.

Middleton, Jo Ann. "Willa Cather and the Fine Reader: A Study of Cather's Techniques and Use of the Void in the Evocation of Reader Response." Ph.D. diss., Drew University, 1987.

Moseley, Ann. "The Voyage Perilous: Willa Cather's Mystic Quest." Ph.D. diss., University of Oklahoma, 1974.

Ostwalt, Conrad Eugene, Jr. "The Secularization of American Space: The Fiction of Willa Cather and Theodore Dreiser." Ph.D. diss., Duke University, 1987.

Plunkett, Kevin Michael. "The Symbol of the Frontier in Selected Novels of Willa Cather." Ph.D. diss., University of Rhode Island, 1982.

Schmittlein, Albert Edward. "Willa Cather's Novels: An Evolving Art." Ph.D. diss., University of Pittsburgh, 1962.

Throckmorton, Jean Lavon. "Willa Cather: Artistic Theory and Practice (Volumes I and II)." Ph.D. diss., University of Kansas, 1954.

Whittington, Charles Calvin, Jr. "The Use of Insert Narrative in the Novels of Willa Cather." Ph.D. diss., Vanderbilt University, 1972.

Yongue, Patricia Lee. "The Immense Design: A Study of Willa Cather's Creative Process." Ph.D. diss., University of California at Los Angeles, 1972.

Index